Pretty Babies

Pretty Babies

An Insider's Look at the World of the Hollywood Child Star

by Andrea Darvi

McGraw-Hill Book Company

NEW YORK   ST. LOUIS   SAN FRANCISCO
TORONTO   HAMBURG   MEXICO

1 2 3 4 5 6 7 8 9 D O C D O C 8 7 6 5 4 3

ISBN 0-07-015402-3

Library of Congress Cataloging in Publication Data

Darvi, Andrea.
Pretty babies.
1. Darvi, Andrea.   2.Moving-picture actors and actresses—United States—Biog-
raphy.   3. Children as actors.   I. Plate, Thomas Gordon.   II. Title.
PN2287.D29A36   1983   791.43'028'0924 [B]   83-10642
ISBN 0-07-015402-3

Book design by Levavi & Levavi

Contents

Acknowledgments

Many thanks to the following sources: Linda Blair, Bobby Burgess, Diana Serra Cary, Kevin Corcoran, Quinn Cummings, Richard Donner, Peggy Ann Garner, Darlene Gillespie, Darryl Hickman, Dwayne Hickman, Earl Hamner, Norman Lear, Dick Moore, Kristy McNichol, Jerry Mathers, Jay North, Margaret O'Brien, Mickey Rooney, Tom Rettig, Mark Rydell, Allison Smith, and Jane Withers. Although it is impossible to thank all the other persons who were most generous with their time, I am especially grateful to Sir David English, the Editor of the London *Daily Mail*, who initially encouraged me to tell this story.

To my parents, Samuel and Evelyn Margolis, who saved the diaries I kept as a Hollywood child actress, and who saved the life that followed.

A special thank-you to my husband,
Thomas Plate, for his editing.

"Success is the necessary misfortune of life, but it is only to the very unfortunate that it comes early."

Anthony Trollope,
Orley Farm (1862)

Preview

I do not want you to think I was excessively competitive. I do not believe I was any worse in this regard than the other children against whom I had to compete. But Hollywood, my first employer, was always quite clear about its demands. Before long, its values became yours. At my first casting call, conducted on a back lot at Warner Brothers Studios in Burbank, dozens of erstwhile and actual child actresses, all dressed to their baby teeth in petticoat regalia, auditioned for a walk-on part. Following the casting director's instructions, each child was to run up to him, holler "Mommy, Mommy," then rush off. Halfway through the line of tiny auditioners, the director of the film, which was already in production elsewhere on the lot, came to watch. It was my turn. Trembling inside, but struggling to remain visibly composed, I sprinted to the center of the stage, smiled broadly at the director, and opened my mouth wide. My first audition, possibly my big break . . . but nothing would come out; I had forgotten the line. "Thank you," whispered the casting director, politely. "Next!" I did not take it well, I admit. The curt dismissal, though clearly justified by my bumbling performance, struck me as a personal rejection. What was wrong with *me*, I wondered on the long, silent drive home? When my mother parked the car in the driveway and opened the door, I refused to follow her inside the house. "Andrea, don't be ridiculous!" she said. I would not move from the car. "It wasn't your fault," she said. No reply. Powerless to get me to react at all, she stormed into the house and left me sitting in the car. Hour after hour I sat there, thinking about where I had gone wrong, if I really had what it takes. My stomach rolled over many times. As darkness fell, I got frightened of being alone, sneaked into the house and tiptoed down the hall to my bedroom. I closed the door behind me and did not speak or come out for hours. This happened when I was six.

I was once a Hollywood child actress. I worked from the ages of seven through thirteen (1959–1965), in both television and movies. I was comparatively lucky; the television industry then was not the quasi-mass industry it is now. The Andrea Darvi story was written on the sets of such quality shows as *Playhouse 90*, *General Electric Theater*, and *The Twilight Zone*. Some of my adult colleagues, whose kindnesses, instructions and warmth I still cherish, were among the finest talents of any era. I worked with pros like Barbara Stanwyck, Art Carney, Boris Karloff, Rod Serling and Alfred Hitchcock. Still, like most child actresses then and now, I was exploited, rejected, and subjected to work pressures that would have collapsed the composure of a thirty year old, much less a preteen. My ego, as well as my make-up, sometimes melted under studio lights, and my relationships with my parents and sister became strained and sometimes stormy. I started at six, was washed up by my early teens and, a professional journalist at thirty, still cannot forget about the experience.

I will tell the story of journeyman child actress Andrea Darvi as best I can, but the more important story in this book concerns the tens of thousands of young children making movies, TV shows and commercials today. Hollywood is both a town and an industry that, much like Detroit, has always symbolized a special kind of American tradecraft, as quintessentially American as fast food and the fast buck. Since the earliest days of the industry, Hollywood has been about the only continuing enterprise in America in which infants and children are gainfully and legally employed at so early an age. But now more than ever, children are assemblyline products of the profitable Hollywood dream machine. In 1982, between 750 and 900 work permits for actual and potential child actors and actresses were dispensed in Los Angeles . . . each month! The growth curve is skyward. In 1978, there were some 11,000 children between the ages of fifteen days and eighteen years employed by Hollywood, mostly as actors and actresses. In 1980, the number had risen to 15,000.

In the seventies and eighties, Hollywood kids did not exactly come of age (Shirley Temple got there first!) but more of them than ever before certainly came into their own. Whether Brooke Shields, who became a movie actress on the heels of her success as a fashion model; or Kristy McNichol, who propelled herself to the movie screen from the initial launching pad of TV commercials (with a very successful four-year stopover in the hit ABC-TV series *Family,* 1976–1980); or Ricky Schroder, who made his name on celluloid in *The Champ* (1979) before becoming the star of the NBC-TV sit-com *Silver Spoons* (1982–), the paths to glory are numerous and more varied than ever before. Actors and actresses like Drew Barrymore and Henry Thomas in *E.T.* (1982), Jodie Foster in *Taxi Driver* (1976), Tatum O'Neal in *Paper Moon* (1973), and Linda Blair in *The Exorcist* (1973) all attest to the contemporary omnipresence of children in Hollywood and are certainly child superstars in the public eye. But from Hollywood's perspective, they are not so much Mickey Rooneys or Shirley Temples or pioneers of any kind as they are, simply, more accessorized and souped-up models of the industry's hottest current assemblyline product, compact division—the child actor.

one

Move Over, Shirley Temple

In 1959, I took my place in a Hollywood tradition that was already more than forty years old. Even in the days of silent films, kids came up fast. There were stars like Baby Marie Osborne (*Little Mary Sunshine*, 1916), Wesley Barry (*Rebecca of Sunnybrook Farm*, 1971), the Fox Kiddies, and the million-dollar Baby Peggy Montgomery (*Playmates*, 1920; *The Kid Reporter*, 1921; *Hansel and Gretel*, 1922). (She was granted the high honor of being the Democratic National Convention mascot in 1924). The silent film era also marked the beginning of the Hal Roach "Our Gang" series that boosted the careers of child actors like George ("Spanky") McFarland, Dick (Dickie) Moore, Darla Hood, Bobby Blake (adult actor Robert Blake) and Jackie Cooper.

Like most child actors of the TV generation in my day and today, however, I had virtually no sense of the historical context in which I worked. Still, I instinctively knew that my predecessors in the field were far more famous, and led more glamourous lives, than average working kids like me. It seemed unfathomable, not to mention unfair, that Charlie Chaplin picked a little boy named Jackie Coogan to star opposite him in *The Kid* (1921), and that afterwards that boy became one of the highest paid stars in America. And to have legislation named after him too![1] It was stupefying to think that Shirley Temple (*Stand Up and Cheer*, 1934; *Little Miss Marker*, 1934) was a top box office hit at seven years old—my age when I was just starting out. As author Diana Serra Cary, formerly the silent film star Baby Peggy, told me, "We were cherished. Children were more important then, because there were not so many to go around. We were constantly exposed to the media and were developed as personality stars as distinctive as Crawford and Garbo." But after the forties, the child superstar of the dimensions of a Mickey Rooney, Judy Garland or Margaret O'Brien was becoming an endangered species. With the decline of the studios in the late forties and fifties, the state of the child actors' industry began to deteriorate. No longer did each studio tend to a small hybrid crop of resident child stars. Child actors would never regain the sense of security and professional stature of the Rooneys and Garlands. Today, for all the Kristy McNichols, Ricky Schroders and Gary Colemans, there are hordes of equally ambitious unknowns. The sheer volume of them has changed the quality of the experience. "Stories were chosen with me and Shirley Temple in mind," says ex-child star Jane Withers (*Bright Eyes*, 1934). "Today, they look for kids to fit the roles. They're all plastic, stamped out of a mold. They look and dress alike. It's like they're on an assemblyline."

With the rising popularity of television in the fifties, a curious paradox arose: job opportunities for children increased, but their stature in the profession began to wane. The television series had a peculiarly dehumanizing effect. Unlike their predecessors in the movie field, children became ensemble players to be seen and remembered only in the contexts of their series. Shows like *Father Knows Best* (1954–1963), that portrayed happy, affluent middle-class American families, spawned a less whole-

---

[1]See the discussion of the Coogan Act, Chapter Two.

some phenomenon—the TV child has-been. The end of the series often meant the end of the child's career. Jay North was acceptable to the American public in only one major role—Dennis the Menace. Most people today can barely remember Johnnie Whitaker, Jody in *Family Affair* (1966–1971), or his former costar, Anissa Jones (Buffy), unless they recall her tragic death from a drug overdose at the age of eighteen. And forty years from now, we will almost certainly fail to remember a Missy Gold (*Benson*, 1979–) as vividly as we do, say, Natalie Wood in *Miracle on 34th Street* (1947), because by then the Hollywood factory will have churned out a brand new line of TV child stars. As Diana Serra Cary remarked, "At least in my day, no one would have said, 'Move over, Shirley Temple.' "

The chorus line of present and future child stars now stretches as far as the eye can see. In the late sixties and early seventies, a number of highly successful family TV series came into being: *The Brady Bunch* (1969–1974), *The Waltons* (1972–1981), *Eight Is Enough* (1977–1981). The seventies also brought forth the better quality, Norman Lear-style sit-com TV in which the top stars were at first adults (whether Carroll O'Connor as Archie Bunker or Bea Arthur as Maude). But by mid-decade, Lear had produced two hit shows featuring children, *Good Times* (1974–1979) and *One Day at a Time* (1975–), and the child actor assemblyline moved into high gear. By the fall of 1982, nine new series revolving around central characters who are children made it to prime time.

When the child actor revolution hit Hollywood, no one was surprised, certainly not Norman Lear. Said the godfather of some of the most successful contemporary shows featuring children (*The Facts of Life*, 1980–; *Square Pegs*, 1982–; *Diff'rent Strokes*, 1978–), "If something works down the street, networks number two and three will copy it. If two kids work with one mother, they will do four kids with two mothers, or eight kids and four mothers." In the entertainment business, a revolution tends to be the product not of originality, but imitation. Like Detroit, Hollywood will react to the hot new car by producing as many copycat versions as the market will absorb.

The benefits to the child actor and his parents are enormous. Besides many good-paying series opportunities, he is in greater demand than ever for TV commercials, which are often better paying. Digging a spoon into a bowl of Rice Krispies or singing to a plate of Spaghettios for a few seconds is not exactly a part on *Playhouse 90* or *Hill Street Blues*. But the monetary rewards are hardly childlike.

There are two opportunity-rich periods for the Hollywood kid. The second begins at the age of six, which agents call "the magic age," when California labor regulations ease and hundreds of children, who had been almost unemployable after fifteen or eighteen months of age, are suddenly back in business. (See Chapter Three, where we discuss this first-period phenomenon.) Preparation for the comeback may begin as soon as age four, when the child is old and articulate enough to make the interview rounds, gaining exposure, confidence and poise to enhance success at six. From six to ten, the job offers may start to come in steadily. After age ten, however, children's employability dwindles because "they're not cute anymore," as one Hollywood agent after another will put it. Ads in Hollywood trade magazines today celebrate this ripe period with photographs of adorable, broadly grinning boys and girls; the captions below often read, "Hurray, I'm six now!"

During this six-to-ten-year-old period, the most employable child is the blonde, blue-eyed, WASPy all-American-looking kid whom agents describe variously as the "P and G" (Proctor and Gamble), "wholesome," or "noncommittal" type. Used in commercials to sell everything from toothpaste to Cheerios, he or she can easily fit into an all-American TV family composed of other all-American children and adults. The kids are usually fitted to the adults, with no room left for imagination in casting. In the minds of most producers, directors and casting personnel, if the parents are blonde, the kids must also be blonde. No one in Hollywood seems to have paid any attention to the recessive-genes lecture in biology class.

Nevertheless, in this business good looks are not as important as the right look; a stigma is sometimes attached to the characterless pretty face, as if the model were all exterior body and no performance. "Very pretty kids are too sterile," says Hollywood agent Iris Burton. Even in commercials, knockout looks can prove a handicap. "When I interview a young Elizabeth Taylor, I shy away from her," says one Los Angeles based commercial director. "They don't like kids who might take away from the product. The theory of advertising is: go for the less beautiful child." Even minority children have a chance to make it now. "No one wants to project an image of prejudice, or to be doubted in terms of the authenticity of their show," says Eve Brandstein, Vice-President, Talent and Casting for Norman Lear's Embassy Communications, who casts a number of shows featuring children. Of course, equal opportunity only goes for as long as the Nielsen ratings hold up.

When I was a child actress, my looks were all wrong— Shirley Temple blonde remained in demand. Hollywood looked at equal opportunity as a bizarre, far-off legal concept in some civil rights agitator's mind. In effect, I became a highly employable stand-in for Hispanics, Indians, Hawaiians and other minorities. When the industry needed a dark ethnic little girl of whatever allegedly obscure racial, historical, or geographical background, Andrea Darvi, an olive-complected, dark-haired, dark-eyed kid with a talent for faking a wide variety of accents and dialects on command, would likely be in business. Given an exotic Hawaiian muumuu, a trail-worn pair of squaw boots or a dusty Mexican poncho, I could and did play virtually any minority type, except black. I was not just frequently cast, I was invariably typecast, though not without reward. What wonderfully challenging character roles I got! On *The Twilight Zone* Andrea Darvi was the Mexican waif pleading passionately to the townspeople to spare her drunken brother from being strung up for a murder he never intended to commit. On *Peter Gunn*, she was an Italian girl who watches in horror as a criminal whom she has befriended is chased by cops and prepares to jump out of a window; on *Hawaiian Eye*, a girl abandoned by her amnesiac father; on *Bonanza*, a half-breed Shoshone Indian trapped inside her home when the white man breaks in; and on the long-running *Combat!* show, a French, war-torn orphan cradled in the arms of the all but invincible Sergeant Saunders, played by the late Vic Morrow. The looks that I had (basic Third World vulnerable) required a modicum of genuine acting ability. Few roles were trifling walk-ons; most were cry-ons (real drama roles).

Children who do dramatic work in TV or film today must have good reading skills, an ability to memorize and, at the very least, the capability to elevate dialogue from the realm of singsong. Hardly any of that is necessary for TV commercials, which generally require no more than an ability to smile widely and speak clearly with a mouth full of food. The days of the thirties and forties, with their plethora of great, multi-talented child stars, are past. Kids in either sit-coms or commercials are not expected to sing like Judy Garland, dance like Shirley Temple, or act like Margaret O'Brien. Darryl Hickman was a very successful and gifted child actor of the forties in movies like *The Grapes of Wrath* (1940), *Boys Ranch* (1946), and *Men of Boys' Town* (1941). Today an adult actor (*Network*, 1976; *Sharky's Machine*, 1981), he put it well: "Talent is only part of it. Say they're looking for a freckle-faced kid with blonde hair to be the son of the star. So you're a blonde-haired kid with a freckled face, you read the lines and you get the job. That doesn't necessarily mean you're a professional actor." Kids like Ricky Schroder, Drew Barrymore and the now adult Kristy McNichol, whose talent we all admire, are exceptions that prove this rule.

One main reason so many children and parents are eager to make it in the entertainment business is the money. Consider the payoff for TV commercials alone. For one day of shooting, the pay may only be $300, but the residuals can prove to be a fortune, depending upon a variety of factors such as whether the commercial is regional or national, how often it is shown and over how long a period of time, and how tough the child's agent may be. For just ten jobs, ten one-day sessions of whining over errant pork sausages or drooling like a rabid dog over a bowl of cereal, a child might earn between $25,000 and $200,000.

A McDonald's commercial today pays the child roughly $3000. A "kiddie ghetto" commercial that is run repeatedly on Saturday mornings between cartoons pays some $7000. There are also "holding fees." This means that for every run of thirteen consecutive weeks, the child receives a check in the amount of $300 to ensure that he will not accept a commercial offer from a competing advertiser. These fees are usually paid to cover a one-year hold, although in unusual cases they have been extended over periods of up to seven years. Although adults are as a rule better paid than children, there is no inherent wage differential on the basis of age within the child actor class. A good diaper commercial with a five- or six-month run pays roughly $5000–7000, while those that run several years are worth at least $10,000.

The pay for TV shows and movies will vary widely, involving such considerations as the child's level of experience and the importance of the role. The child with little or no prior experience who lands a series may, in his first year, earn $2500–$3000 per week, for a twenty-six-week-a-year run. The child with a seven-year series contract should get yearly raises of at least $500 per week. To land in a long-running series like *The Waltons* (1972–1981) or *Little House on the Prairie* (1974–), winding up in the $5000–6000-a-week range, means the child can become financially secure for life. Even sporadic, episodic work pays well. On a job where the shooting runs five days (the average length of time it takes to complete a half-hour show), even a rank newcomer can make at least $1250–1500; for a major role in an hour-long show, the minimum price could be roughly $1600. These figures are conservative. In 1982, even the tightly budgeted hour-long show cost an average of $640,000 to produce; a half-hour comedy perhaps could be done for $350,000.

There are plenty of things besides money that children love about the entertainment business: the exposure to exciting and important people; having a creative outlet that is far more stimulating than the daily routine at school; the opportunity to travel for free; and the attention they get. As eleven-year-old Sydney Penny (NBC's *The Capture of Grizzly Adams*, 1982; ABC's *The Thorn Birds*, 1983) told me, "I've thought being a horse trainer wouldn't be as much fun as being an actress in front of a crowd. Not a lot of horse trainers sign autographs." A lot of children are truly enthusiastic about their burdgeoning careers. "Acting is fun," one after another will say, although they seem unable to distinguish fun from success. "Interviews are fun because they give you a chance to be on TV," says twelve-year-old Shane Butterworth (*Exorcist II: The Heretic*, 1977; *Bad News Bears*, 1979–1980). "Telethons are fun because if a director watching one sees me, that can change my whole career around." Kids like him are driven by an overwhelming desire to succeed in the business and are sure of only one thing—they do not want to fail. Said eleven-year-old Jennifer Horton, a commercial protegé who at the time we met had gotten her first dramatic role playing Linda Gray's daughter in the 1982 CBS-TV movie *Not in Front of the Children*, "I am interested in *getting parts*. I want to make it and be a great or even a small movie star." Children who act are made to want recognition and success as quickly as possible by the circumstances of being a child actor or actress; they know their biological timeclocks are forever ticking away, from the first moments in the spotlight.

For all the rewards, children pay a high price. Says Linda Blair, now in her twenties, "You have to grow up early. I've been working and supporting myself since I was six years old. I missed going to Daddy and saying, 'Give me money, I want to go off and do this or that.' I competed with kids whose parents supported them. It was very hard. I paid my dues. I was never carefree."

No child actor is allowed to be a child. Kids who expect to be babied and pampered along the way will not make it. The way to get a job is to sell oneself on an interview—no easy feat. Post-toddler-age children are required to make the rounds carting thick portfolios crammed full of commercial studio shots and stills taken on various jobs, as well as résumés listing their credits and areas of specialization: singing, dancing, acrobatics, etc. Like adults in the field, kids feel the intense professional pressure. The business demands sacrifice. "I always wanted to go to parties and play with my girlfriends," says Blair. "That's why I took it on myself in later years to be my own self. I wasn't going to let anything stop me a second time."

If the judicious mother will not drag her child to cattlecalls day after day, the ambitious one will. The competition for jobs is fierce. Parents know they may have to gamble away months, years, even an entire childhood, before hitting a jackpot. The hottest TV-commercial child averages only one job in every twenty or thirty interviews. For most, the odds are more like forty to one. Says Hollywood casting director Sheila Manning, "No one does better than one in five."

Interview dread, like stage fright, can be cured with a little experience. "I used to get nervous when I was about four or five," one upcoming nine-year-old actor told me. "I was afraid I'd mess up." The fear is most understandable. Consider the child who arrives at an interview with one hundred or more kids and mothers spilling onto the sidewalk down a block or two in a mad mob scene. For a TV commercial, if the advertiser has given the casting director who is conducting the interview detailed specifications (blondes but not tow-heads; red-heads with no freckles; kids with dark but not black hair), the casting office will look like a factory of kiddie clones.

Not surprisingly, Hollywood kids find the big commercial calls demeaning. Sometimes they are seen for just seconds at a time—one quick shot in front of a videotape machine, and they are dismissed. Only on callbacks are they required to read the script. At one such callback for a Kellogg's commercial that I observed, a casting director, fishing for the right combination of kids, reeled in groups of three at a time for several hours. Before videotaping their performances, she would direct them in the group scene, urging them to deliver their lines with an overabundance of enthusiasm to an imaginary Snap, Crackle and Pop (played by two toy soldiers and a jar of hand lotion). Seated behind a table with a real box of cereal (heaven forbid the product itself be a fake!), straw baskets serving as cereal bowls and the makeshift animated characters, she would say, "Relate to Snap, Crackle and Pop. . . . And remember, the other kids are your best friends. You're all having a good time." Those who were able to pull it off had to be top talents: most kids have a miserable time on calls like this and would rather kill off the competition than befriend it. "You've got to go in and give them this phony smile," fifteen-year-old Pat Petersen (*Knots Landing*, 1979–) complained. Says Sydney Penny, wise beyond her years, "On a cereal commercial, they want you to look playful and awkward and to hold your spoon like it's a baseball bat because that's considered all-American. But if *I* got a commercial, I'd hold my spoon that way too."

Interviewers may like children who are polite, but agents coach them to be pushy—give it your all, show them what you've got, they hammer into you. Some kids have difficulty walking that tightrope. I certainly did. At the age of eleven, after having auditioned for a part on the TV series *The Fugitive* (1963–1967), I wrote in my diary, "I was sort of embarrassed because when they asked me how long I was acting, I told them they should look at my book of pictures and credits. The casting man laughed and I think maybe the producer smiled. Then the director said, 'I'll look at your book. I think little girls who bring their credits in should have them seen.' " Not everyone might have found my lack of graciousness so charming. As British director Jack Clayton (*Room at the Top*, 1959; *The Great Gatsby*, 1974) put it, "The Hollywood kid? All you have to do is say something like, 'What school do you go to?' Or 'What sports do you like?' and the child supplies all the dialogue. Before you get your questions together, he has gone over his whole career without leaving one moment of silence. That's my impression of a Hollywood kid."

Lying is another part of the Hollywood kid's standard repertoire. For instance, you are taught to make yourself younger to seem like a prodigy, or to seem perfectly suited to the character being cast, or to keep them from noticing that you are becoming an ancient thirteen year old. In car rides to the studios, my mother used to coach me to memorize a phony birthdate in the unlikely event that they would try to trap me. Maybe no one likes a child who lies, but the system encourages it. In a highly competitive industry swarming with ambitious mothers, agents and kids, lying is a survival tool. When I observed the stream of kids trying out for the Kellogg's commercial, I noticed one little girl shout out cheerily, "I'm six now!"—adding a moment later, "No, I'm seven!" She was probably eight.

Whether six or twelve, child actors and actresses are forced to become miniature adults. When I auditioned for a part in a movie entitled *Little Girl Lost,* producer Harold Lloyd Jr., determined to test whether or not I had the fortitude to do the scene requiring the little girl to swim in the ocean with dolphins, affected a tone of voice he considered appropriately childlike and asked point blank, "Do you like to swim with dolphins?" To which I answered matter-of-factly, "I don't know. I've never had the experience." Everyone in the room roared, but I really wasn't going for laughs; I just wanted the part. Jerry Mathers says that he may have won the title role in the popular *Leave It to Beaver* television series (1957–1963) by giving his interviewers the impression of an almost mature perspective on opportunity. "Since they called me right after school to one of the last callbacks, I went in wearing my Cub Scout uniform," he remembers. "They saw I was fidgety and asked, 'What's wrong?' I said, 'I've been here several times and the sooner I get out of here, I can get to my Cub Scout meeting.' They must have wanted someone who didn't really want to work, someone not so anxious."

That is surely a rare quality among today's Hollywood kids. Getting a part is an unforgettable high. I can still recall the surge of joy that would come to me when a messenger from the principal's office entered the classroom with a note for me that read, "Call home at once." I knew that meant triumph. Or when I would catch sight of my mother standing on the sidewalk outside the school playground at recess. Beckoning to me from the other side of the chain-link fence while I ran to her, she would yell out, "You got it!" A warm, loving, congratulatory smile would fill her face. Suddenly I was transported from the dull, insignificant world of school to the glamour and glory of Hollywood.

But when you don't get the part? "Rejection helps children become more stable," one agent and mother of a former child actress told me, reiterating a popular line of logic in Hollywood circles. "Then they can take rejection as adults." It is an utterly absurd hypothesis. At that early age, enrichment is rarely a product of being spurned. As topnotch former child star Kristy McNichol, who regrets the risks she had to take to get where she is today, puts it, "It's very hard on a child's feelings. There are a lot of people pulling at you. This business has done very well by me, but it is also very chancey that it will go well."

The only way to survive is to compete, with a vengeance. Ruth Withers used to tell her daughter Jane, "Always remember, no matter how good you are, there's somebody a little better just waiting to take your place. Don't you ever forget it." Says Jane, some forty years later, "I never have." The drive to succeed cannot be turned on and off easily. Like many child actors, I grew up regarding all other children not as friends and playmates but as competitors of whom I had better be wary. But I was probably no more driven than any reasonably successful child actress. Allison Smith, the fourth child to play the title role in *Annie* on Broadway, starring in the show for over two years, told me, "I've seen some kids who didn't get parts hit their heads on the wall and stomp their feet." She also told me how desperately the other girls playing orphans in *Annie* wanted their shot at the title role. I then remarked, "Don't you wish you could give them a chance?" Allison swiftly replied, "*No way.*" This is the mentality of the determined child actress.

One who works steadily must learn to function at a fairly ferocious pace. It is quite common for a Little League devotée to wind up slipping into his uniform in the backseat of the car after a full day's shooting while his mother races over the freeway from the studio to the playing field, or out of uniform as he is rushed from the pitcher's mound to a late-afternoon interview. Then home . . . to wash off make-up, memorize the next day's lines, and try to get a good night's rest. Saturday mornings and afternoons are not the beginning of a relaxing weekend. Those are the times usually reserved for acting, singing or dancing lessons. Friends have to wait in line.

The child actor on Broadway has it particularly rough. Long-term stage work is grueling. Most Broadway houses are lit up eight times a week. Compared to television series, movies or commercials, theatrical work is low paying. Scale pay for performers of all ages is under $600 a week. And stage children must have exceptional stamina. "The most successful ones are the tough ones," says Broadway *Annie* lyricist and director Martin Charnin. "Some kids are very gifted, but they're not strong enough. Character is important." Despite all the problems, New York agents encourage kids to go Broadway. "It looks great on a résumé," explains agent Judy Klein. "It means you're really talented." In addition, the child appearing in a long-running hit like *Annie* builds a name and is continually seen.

The story of twelve-year-old Jennine Babo, who at the time we met had been playing one of the orphans in the Broadway production of *Annie* for four grueling years, illustrates the point. She was ideally suited to the work. She never once complained when, at the age of seven, she was uprooted from her home in Bucks County, Pennsylvania, and placed on the Broadway stage. After attending public school in the first grade, she was educated exclusively by private tutors. "I guess I'll stay in it until I grow out of the part," she told me, a tone of good-natured resignation to her voice. (After a long run of over 4 years, the show closed.) On performance days, Wednesdays through Sundays, she and her mother existed in a small, dark, drab studio apartment located on Eighth Avenue and Fifty-second Street, a block around the corner from the theater. On Mondays they would hop on a train back to Bucks County to visit the two boys in the family back home.

Whether on Broadway or in Hollywood, the home of the child actor is no idyllic scene from *Family*. The living room becomes a Green Room, and even if only one child is in the entertainment business, the involvement becomes a family-wide obsession. Jerry Mathers was the uncontested star among his three brothers and one sister who dabbled in the business, and all the Mathers children focused their lives around Jerry's success. When he was invited to Hawaii to appear at the opening of a retail store, the studio financed a two-week-long vacation in the tropical paradise for the entire family of seven. In most cases, even within the home, when the star of the family is on TV all routine activities come to an abrupt halt. Ten minutes before the show is about to come on, the parents set up the videotape machine so as to preserve the performance for posterity. In many family screening rooms, a second television is turned on just in case, heaven forbid, one suddenly goes on the blink. When the program begins, the living room grows as silent as a chapel. When the commercial comes on, the room instantly erupts into a noisy celebration of the star in its midst. "It was an *event*," remembers ex-Mouseketeer Darlene Gillespie. "Everyone stared at the set, transfixed. The phone would be taken off the hook during the entire show. Then afterwards it would ring . . . and it would be neighbors, friends, the agent. . . . My mother was the one who always talked to them." Remembers her sister Larrian, with whom I once worked on an episode of *The Twilight Zone*, "She'd say, 'Didn't she really get to you?' Or, 'Wasn't that crying scene great?' "

These moments of sharing may temporarily bring the family together, but on the whole, the Hollywood child's career puts pressures on family life that tend to pull it apart. My own father loved the glamour and excitement of the entertainment world. He relished the stories and gossip about stars that my mother and I conveyed at the dinner table. But he was an unusually tolerant husband, as my mother herself acknowledged many years after my career had ended. "Only he would accept whatever I threw on the table," she told me. "We didn't entertain, never went anywhere, and had no social life because I had no time. I worked hard for my child, and when I came home I was tired. I could have been a better wife. Yes, I was neglectful."

In this era of double-digit unemployment, when the acting child may bring in more money than either parent, reliance upon him as a breadwinner can sow the seeds of severe marital discord. Consider the situation in which the nine- or ten-year-old child makes more money in a week than his father earns in a month. Rather than face up to the humiliation of being second-best, the father takes a walk. No great loss. As Hollywood agent Evelyn Schultz told me, thinking about some of the families that have been split apart by her clients' newfound good fortune, "The mother has a child who can support her better, so she thinks, 'Who needs him?' "

Intense sibling rivalries are often created when only one child is a professional actor. Under the most normal conditions, children must struggle to negotiate their relationships with their parents; but the negotiations become torturous if the parents are constantly centering their attentions on the child who is often on a movie or TV set. Says New York-based child psychiatrist Richard Atkins, who has treated several severe cases of emotional maladjustment suffered by the siblings of child actors, "The emphasis of parenting is switched to the child star, who is adored. It would be like if Jesus Christ had a brother." Says Dolores Jacoby, referring to her brood of five, "It's hard to be fair to all your children. I don't think Gypsy Rose Lee's mother was bad. She just showered more attention on June than on Louise. Louise took it wrong and thought she loved June more." Mothers are the last to admit they might be incapable of ironing out their children's Hollywood-created conflicts. But anyone who knows the first thing about the competitive nature of the entertainment industry must regard any such disclaimers as preposterous. As Dr. Michael Mantell, former chief psychologist of Children's Hospital in San Diego, California, who has interviewed a number of child performers, told me, "Sibling rivalry in and of itself, after all, is normal. Sometimes there is an educational process going on, a silent understanding between the parents and children, implying, 'We won't talk about the problems.' The kids know the equilibrium of the family will be much too upset if they talk."

If kids won't talk about it, some mothers, unfortunately, will. There was one four-year-old girl struggling to perform up to par on a mosquito repellent commercial. Her lines called for her to cry because of a bad bug bite. But she was so happy to be working at all that everytime the cameras rolled, she popped onto the set smiling, instead of crying. "She had her finger on the place where she was supposed to be bitten, but she was beaming as though the mosquito bite were a new diamond ring," remembers a witness on the set. For several hours, the director tried to elicit the look of pain on her face called for by the script; alas, she continued to radiate glee. The girl's mother then intervened, went over to the child and urgently whispered something in her ear. "Action!" the director shouted, and the child made her entrance. This time, the smile everyone thought was unbreakable had vanished, and her eyes were brimming with tears. Within minutes, the commercial was shot, in the can. The director was elated but also curious. What expert technique had the mother employed to make her daughter cry? Explained dear old Mom, "This is the first time she's done TV work, and she's been wanting to do it all her life because she sees her older sister on TV commercials all the time. I said to her, 'Don't worry, darling, we'll call your sister and she can come in and do the job.' "

My own sister, who never got a single role in Hollywood, must have had a very rough time. Like many child actors with unsuccessful siblings, I privately suspected that each of my successes magnified her sense of failure. I even began to feel guilty for the good fortune in my life, but not guilty enough to want to switch places. As I wrote in my diary on September 23, 1964, when my sister, then eighteen, was selected to dance on *The Danny Kaye Show*, "I am jealous. This time it was her that Mommy spoke about to Aunt Adrian and I got little attention. I don't know how she stands it when I work."

There are two sides to every story. Like a lot of child actresses, I endured a good deal of heartache, but I also experienced some wonderful moments. There *are* definite advantages to having been through it all. Like child actors before and after my time, I had, by the tender age of thirteen, enjoyed the kind of career and sense of accomplishment that adults four times my age could only dream about. I had the opportunity to travel, and to work intimately with creative minds and fantastic talents. It was not only educational, it was fun.

The rigors of the entertainment business help build a child's discipline, work habits and powers of concentration. He learns how to be aggressive, articulate, socially graceful—qualities that enhance lifelong success. Children who are exposed to the workings of this adult world do acquire invaluable knowledge, however painful the lessons. As a rule, if there is one thing an ex-child actor does well, it is to perform on a professional level. He is an expert trained at the dynamics of interviewing and selling himself. He perseveres. He is strong. Learning the business by osmosis at an early age, the ex-child actor can turn to writing, directing and producing, oftentimes with relative ease. And in any business, the former child star with a big name can use it to his advantage, although some find this exploitation emotionally difficult to manage. Dick (Dickie) Moore, one of the stars of the "Our Gang" comedies and of major movies like *Oliver* (1933), now in his fifties and running his own New York-based public relations firm, told me it took many years to feel comfortable capitalizing on his fame as Dickie Moore, former child star. "You end up competing with a self that no longer exists," he says. "That's a very fragmenting experience, in terms of your whole internal psyche. You think, how important am I now? What kind of billing am I getting? It creates a sense of anxiety that's always there in your adult life."

While it lasts, the child actor's career is an acceptable, even wonderful, commitment of time and energy. But the child is father to the man, mother to the woman; the long-range consequences of a child actor's career need to be carefully examined. "I didn't really have a childhood," Kristy McNichol told me on the eve of her twentieth birthday. "It's not that I don't care, it's just that, if I didn't have it, what can I do about it? I can't be a child now." And then, as if putting a barrier around the realization that the past over which she had no control was at least in part a serious mistake, she added, "I'm kind of glad

I didn't have one [a childhood]. I think the earlier you learn about life and working, money and situations that you have to deal with later anyways, the better off you'll be. Why wait? . . . But if it were my child, I would probably not want it to be in the movie industry. I'd let my child make its own decisions. If I were financially stable, I'd send it to college." It takes the perspective of adulthood to realize that sense of loss. When Brooke Shields, seventeen, appeared on *The Barbara Walters Special* to reassure the country she was having an absolutely wonderful time being a child superstar, she was probably telling the truth as best she understood it then. The long-range question is not: is Brooke Shields happy being on top now? But, when today's triumphs have long been forgotten, will she come to view her early career as a risky investment at too high a cost?

In fact, many ex-child actors have serious misgivings about their past careers. For every Jane Withers and Mickey Rooney swearing never to have regretted a single moment, there are hundreds of others who say they have indeed. Natalie Wood once told a newspaper reporter that for all the benefits and enjoyments she received from her career as a child actress, she was not eager for her children to emulate her. "Let them get a little older," she said. "I don't want them starting so young." She also felt compelled to mention that the psychiatric bills she accumulated in adulthood were "at least the equal of the annual defense budget of most Central American nations." As Darryl Hickman remembers, "I felt an enormous responsibility and psychological need to be supportive of my mother and the family because I sensed that I had a certain kind of talent and capacity to do things that not everyone has. I felt an obligation to use those things, and it really kind of used me up and didn't give me the opportunity to grow up in a way that was entirely healthy. I tend to feel compassion for any child who's acting. It's an untenable position to be in. I've never seen or known anyone, or been privileged with any information or insight, that suggests otherwise." His brother Dwayne (*The Many Loves of Dobie Gillis*, 1959–1963), agrees, "It's an unnatural way of life for a child. It's like asking him to come over to CBS and be an executive like I am now. It has no advantages. I don't know why kids or parents do it."

One does *not* have to be an ex-child actor to have had an unhappy past. These are not children of the Holocaust, or slum kids bitten by rats during the night. Growing up is hard on everyone, and not all cases of teenage suicide involve former child actors. Perhaps Natalie Wood would have had astronomically high psychiatric bills as an adult whether or not she had been a child star. But surely, playing for such high stakes at such an early age is a tremendous jolt.

Director Mark Rydell (*The Rose*, 1979; *On Golden Pond*, 1982) raises an additional point. "It is inevitable, with any child star, that it has to end." The end is almost never sweet. To be made to feel like a useless, washed-up has-been, a failure at fourteen; to see adolescence as an end, instead of a beginning; to be left with little more than a heap of bittersweet memories to cancel out those residual checks—that's Hollywood. "It's inherent in the business to use you until they don't need you," say former child actor Jim (Jimmy) Hawkins (*The Ruggles*, 1949–1952; *Annie Oakley*, 1952–1966). "A kid doesn't understand the rules—but that's the business, whether you're a major star at thirty, forty-eight or eight."

Once the first steps are taken, the child actor's life is almost always irrevocably altered. "You have a normal life, but it's still a different type of life," says Margaret O'Brien (*Journey for Margaret*, 1942; *Meet Me in St. Louis*, 1944). Her somewhat contradictory analysis is easy to understand. The child actor of any era has deep-seated fears of being perceived as a freak. It is a kind of paranoia he inherits from his mother, who has spent years trying unsuccessfully to combat the stigma surrounding child actors and their parents. Mothers teach their children to hide behind the use of vague, meaningless clichés like "normal," "regular," and "average," in the effort to develop self-images that are acceptable to the world at large. But child actors are anything but "average." Average kids do not spend vast amounts of time working with adults, going to school in trailers on studio lots, or making thousands of dollars a week. Average kids do not appear on the screens of televisions and movie houses across the nation. Average kids do not support entire family budgets. Fourteen-year-old Quinn Cummings (*The Goodbye Girl*, 1977; *Family*, 1978–1980), who decided that acting would be her lifelong career at the age of ten, snapped at me, "If I were brought up in a family of writers, no one would question me." This is exactly the point: a child can't become a writer, lawyer, doctor, or any other type of professional, for that matter, so soon after birth . . . but an actor, yes.

Whether or not he is a superstar like Gary Coleman, the Hollywood child leads a life that is unique. This is not due so much to the content of his work as the sharp, unrelenting focus of his mind, and the total investment of his emotions toward a single professional goal. For me, as for many ex-child actors who went on to pursue careers unrelated to the entertainment world, growing up meant unlearning the lessons of childhood. "If I hadn't been a child actor," Mickey Rooney told me, "I would have prayed to God, because I couldn't live without it." How many of us who have tasted success early make such a preposterous claim at some point in our lives! A child actor's sense of self-worth is directly related to the degree of public recognition he receives. When I was only nine years old, I used to tell my mother I would commit suicide if I couldn't act. Six years later, even though I hadn't worked in several years, that conviction remained equally strong. As I wrote at fifteen years of age in my diary in September 1967, "I am different from the average person my age, and always was. I hate school and don't fit in socially, so I long to work. I belong acting, with adults. Other kids may leave a job and that's that, but to me it means so much more, it's *me*." It took a lot of soul-searching, and many years away from Hollywood, to know who I was. And was not.

two

The Mothers' Underground

L ike child actors, Hollywood mothers tend to start early. "When she was fourteen years old," Jane Withers told me, "my mother began to plan that she would grow up, have a wonderful marriage, have one child—a girl—and that girl was going to be very successful in show business. That's *all* she ever planned, worked toward and prayed about. When I was finally expected, she used to go and study marquees. She thought Withers was a long last name and she would have to have a short first one that would look right on the marquee, so she chose Jane.

"When I was two, she would play records by Fifi D'Orsay, a marvelous lady who did impersonations of all the different stars of the time. Mama couldn't play a note on the piano, but with one finger she could play melodies and teach me all the current songs. She would take me to the movies that she felt would be right for me to see. So by the time I was two and a half, I was on the stage doing impersonations of all the different stars I saw: Maurice Chevalier, Rudy Vallee, Mae West, W. C. Fields, Eddie Cantor . . .

"I felt very blessed to be able to live up to my mother's expectations. Mama and I always used to kid. I'd say, 'Dear God, supposing I had arrived with no talent—what would we do? It would be so tacky! You dreamed about this!'

"She thought the entertainment business was a very fascinating and interesting life. It *wasn't* for herself. She was *never* a stage mother.

"My father left my career entirely up to my mother. We came out to California on a six-month trial basis, to see if I could make it. I was only five and a half, but I was known all over the south. I had my own radio show by the time I was three and a half, as Dixie's Dainty Dewdrop in Atlanta, doing impersonations and singing.

"The biggest disappointment of all was when I was called in to be signed for the role in *Stand Up and Cheer* [1934]. I wasn't quite seven at the time. I didn't look like what the part called for. I was really a plain Jane. Mama and I were going in to see Winfield Sheehan, who was then the vice president of Fox. We were sitting in the outer office waiting to be called in to sign the contract. All of a sudden, the door opened, and the most beautiful, adorable, precious child I had ever seen walked through. At that moment, my heart sank—not for my sake, *but for my mother's*. I knew that my mother was going to be terribly upset, because she felt that finally my big moment had come. They had opened the door and said, 'Won't you come in?' Not to us, but to this precious adorable little child. I leaned over to my mother and said, 'Now, Mama, don't you be too disappointed if I don't get this contract.' She said, 'What do you mean, that's what we're here for!' I said, 'I think the little girl who just walked into this office is going to play this role, she's exactly what the part calls for.' She said, 'But you've got the talent!' I said, 'Yes, but maybe it's not my time yet.' I didn't know the little girl's name, but it was Shirley Temple.' "

Less than a year, later, Mrs. Withers' loving dreams for her daughter started to come true. Jane, then seven, landed an important part as the mean kid playing *opposite* Shirley Temple in the movie *Bright Eyes* (1934). Many other successes, like *Gentle Julia* (1936) and *Wild and Woolly* (1937), soon followed. "My mother was my best friend," says Jane. "Everything she ever planned for me became a reality." Even now, when her mother is well into her eighties and in failing health, Jane knows that her career is still uppermost in her mother's mind. "One day the nurses at the private hospital called me and said she was having a very bad spell," says Jane, now in her fifties. "So I went to the hospital [in Los Angeles] where I visit her every day. She was saying over and over to anyone who would listen, 'Jane's on a picture, but I don't know where! I have to be there with her all the time. I have to be on the set, that's the law!' I went in and said, 'Hi, Mom! Isn't it wonderful that I don't have to go to the studio today, it's Sunday! We are going to have a picnic lunch right here.' She said that would be fun, and I fed her her lunch."

Reality is not always so kind to plans, or mothers.

A dozen children stood in line at the center of a playhouse stage in Pasadena, California, nervously facing their hostile audience. The faces of the twelve mothers seated below revealed anxiety, hurt, dread. It is always nerve-wracking to see your child on stage, but on an occasion like this, it can be devastating. The tension in the room heightened as the last in a series of acting lessons for the season drew to a close. The topic of this one: "How *not* to be a Stage Mother."

"Tell your mothers the worst thing you've ever wanted to tell them," the teacher, Hollywood agent Don Schwartz, instructed the children on stage. The line began to open fire. One by one, the children's complaints shot forth like bullets piercing their mothers' hearts:

"Mom, quit pushing me."

"Quit brushing my hair so much."

"You make me nervous!"

After the last child had lobbed his accusation, Schwartz

jokingly announced their final assignment. "Now kick your mothers in the shins and warn them never to be stage mothers again."

The children walked timidly into the audience, then class was dismissed. "Maybe some of them really *did* kick their mothers," Schwartz gleefully speculated afterwards. "So what? Why shouldn't they? Stage mothers are the worst animals alive. If they kick them, more power to them."

If you are a child in the entertainment field, almost everyone assumes that your mother is a carbon copy of the archetypical Hollywood Monster Mother. People both within and outside of the industry are likely to peg her as a pushy, abusive, fire-breathing dragoness willing to sell her child down the river for the promise of a role—not to mention a buck.

But there is a reason why people think this way; the cliché is often true. History offers scant evidence suggesting otherwise. Some stage mothers become as legendary for the parts they play in Hollywood as their children, who, more than anyone else, find their mothers' sideline performances unforgettable. When Judy Garland was in her forties and well into superstardom, the memory of her deceased mother haunted her in ways both comic and tragic. Recalls attorney Godfrey Isaac, who handled two of Judy's divorces, "She had flashes of incredible hatred for her mother. She lived with her mother every day of her life. And if she said anything outlandish, her eyes would roll up, she'd look at the ceiling and say, 'My mother's listening.' "

Many old-time child stars have had celebrated quarrels with their mothers or other close relatives. In her late teens, former child star Peggy Ann Garner (*A Tree Grows in Brooklyn,* 1945; *Jane Eyre,* 1944; *Nob Hill,* 1945) made newspaper headlines when her guardianship was transferred from her mother to her father in a divorce action. Jackie Coogan in 1938 sued his family to recover his earnings. Child stars like Freddie Bartholomew also wound up in court in family battles over their financial gains.

Wars between stage mothers and child actors in Hollywood are always breaking out. Even today, the stereotypical exploitative woman, peddling somewhere between fifty and one hundred youthful pounds of unbounded energy, remains a central figure within the drove of Hollywood mothers. But has the "stage mother" stigma been unjustly exaggerated? Has the cliché become a smear? Is every mother who plays the Hollywood game a "Mommie Dearest"? Alternatively, what percentage are simply hard-working, conscientious women guilty of harboring nothing more terrible than dreams for their children?

The exact concentration of unmitigated stage mothers at all levels of the entertainment industry today is anyone's educated guess, of course. One in a hundred? Two in ten? Five per cent? Name your figure. The only estimate you will not hear in Hollywood is that there is an insignificant number of stage mothers on the prowl these days. As Paramount Studios casting director Bobby Hoffman (*Joanie Loves Chachi*, September–December 1982; *Happy Days*, 1974–; *Laverne and Shirley*, 1976–) told me, "Maybe they're a small minority, but such a strong minority that they stand out."

Mothers make a strong case for themselves. "If not for the stage parent," says Dolores Jacoby, mother of five child actors,[1] "there would be no liaison with the school, no getting to the interviews, no wearing the right clothes, no money saved." Despite the understandable bias, her conclusion is correct. Who else would drive the children to lessons, choose their photographs, keep tabs on their agents, and sit on sets hour after hour?

But while mothers are undeniably the moving forces behind their children's careers, they are curiously reluctant to accept the credit. "It just walked in the door," protested Toni Kelman (today one of the top children's agents in Hollywood), recalling a shouting match that took place more than twenty

[1]Scott Jacoby won an Emmy for his performance in the 1972 ABC-TV movie *That Certain Summer*. Bobby Jacoby is a regular on the TV series *Knots Landing*. Billy Jacoby is a regular on the new TV series *It's Not Easy*. Laura Jacoby appears on another new series, *Mr. Smith*.

years ago with an elementary school principal who had once attacked her for overextending her son. The principal expressed grave reluctance to renew the boy's work permit every six months. Kelman, shaken by the principal's blanket condemnation, felt compelled to offer a self-defense. "I went to rent a house with my three kids," she told me, replaying her conversation with the principal. "As it happened, the woman who owned the house worked for an agent. She saw the kids and said, 'Have you ever thought of letting them work?' I said, 'I'm too busy.' " But the agent, according to Kelman's recollection of events, continued to press the point, and bullied an appointment out of her and her three children. After the initial interview, Kelman said she had qualms about a number of things, including shelling out fifty dollars for beginning promotional photographs. But she was intrigued, so she borrowed the money from her father. "I couldn't tell my *husband* because I was afraid he'd think I was silly," she told the principal. "This was six months before my oldest son, who was then seven, got a call for a Kellogg's commercial interview. He got the job. Then I told my husband when he came home that night, 'Guess what! Your son's going to work!' " Kelman's protestation of innocence was effective; the principal gave up arguing with her and signed her son's work permit.

Serendipity, not Machiavellianism, is the how-my-son-or-daughter-got-started theme of most mothers. As Evelyn Schultz, another contemporary children's agent, put it, she too became a stage mother by sheer accident. A series of "mishaps" some thirty years ago got her six-*week*-old baby twins' movie careers going. "A neighbor across the street had children who were extras in a film," she recalls. "She told somebody in Central Casting about my gorgeous twin boys. They were looking for a good pair for *The Long Gray Line* [1955], with Tyrone Power and Maureen O'Hara. Someone from Central Casting called me. They were in a rush. I agreed, and they sent a limousine to the house. We got work permits that day. The next day the limousine came again and took us to the studio. Filming began right away."

Soon word of the hot new twins in *The Long Gray Line* made the Hollywood rounds. Production officials on the set of *The Untamed* (1955) heard about the pair. Within weeks, the twins were on their way to success. "My kids worked quite a bit as babies," Schultz told me, "just by word of mouth." They kept on working. Later on, she booked them with a children's agent. But then the work started coming for one child or the other, not in tandem. "I loved it, of course," Schultz adds. "I couldn't believe that I was there. John Ford, the famous director, was kissing their feet on the set of *The Long Gray Line*, telling me, 'I can't thank you enough for bringing the boys,' and all I could do was stutter and say, 'I can't thank you enough for our being here.' "

It is easy for mothers to get hooked. The high of that first job is unforgettable. Who can blame them for spending the rest of their lives looking again and again for that fix?

"People say, 'I don't want my child in this business,' " Dolores Jacoby told me. "I think that's baloney. When the mother says that, what she is really saying is she *desperately* wants her child in the business."

Dolores certainly did. She had been scouting around New York for some time, searching for a full-time job to help her husband put aside savings for her children's educations, as well as picking up odd jobs here and there. One day a friend suggested trying her kids at commercials. Tired of waitressing, she was attracted by the glamour of the idea. She succeeded in booking them with an agent, who began sending them on calls. She enrolled them in classes with a drama coach. Her children offered no resistance, and eventually her ten-year-old daughter, Susan, landed an inauspicious nosespray commercial. But the product—and the ad—had a long run; from that one commercial, Susan put away her entire college savings.

Throughout history, child actors have been major family breadwinners, of course. In 1938, the Coogan Act was established, after former child star Jackie Coogan recovered but a pitifully small fraction of his million-dollar earnings in a bitter legal battle with his family. This law states that at least fifty per cent of a child actor's earnings must be put aside in a fund or court-approved savings plan and kept safely until he turns eighteen years old.

But the act offers weak protection. In essence, it only covers those relatively rare contracts that are taken to court for approval by a studio anxious to ensure the child's long-range commitment to the job (i.e., in the case of a series, or, occasionally, a major motion picture). For the majority of child actors, this situation never arises. Fewer and fewer contracts require court processing today. With so many additional kids in the business, more and more work is being done, often for TV commercials, by independent companies that are unfamiliar with all the industry rules and regulations, and sometimes couldn't care less about them.

Some child actors have no idea how much money they make and don't especially care to find out. Money is understandably of no concern to those who have never had to work to survive, and some kids do not have parents of the utmost integrity. "Sometimes my mother borrows a couple of hundred dollars to pay the bills, but it doesn't bother me," one twelve-year-old boy told me. Whenever I asked kids about the financial rewards of their work, their answers were confused and self-conscious. They replied, for example, "I don't think about it. It just goes in the bank"; "I don't do it for the money, although I'd like to have a lot"; "I don't think about the money, but when I do think about it, that's kind of why I'm in it."

What scant information kids may possibly pick up on the Jackie Coogan case has little impact on those who trust their parents. In my case, a warning proffered by Jackie Coogan himself sailed well over my head. One afternoon, when I was eight years old and working on a *General Electric Theater* episode, Coogan wandered onto our set from another one at CBS. Spotting me for the naive child that he himself once was, he walked over and, joking loud enough for everyone to hear, said, "Save your money, kid, save your money!"

The entertainment business is still unresolved about how to settle Coogan-related issues. Just recently, the Screen Actors

Guild Children's Committee in Hollywood proposed that parents be required to put in trust a substantial percentage of the child actor's earnings, based on a sliding scale of income as reported to the Internal Revenue Service. The proposal has met with strong opposition from many parents, however. They argue that such changes in legislation are unfair, and that one must take into consideration the heap of business expenses necessarily incurred, whether for photographs, lessons, agents' and managers' fees, gasoline, wear-and-tear on the car, union dues and so on. In addition, many parents in Hollywood are now arguing that it is not necessarily *wrong* for parents to be supported by their kids. Consider the plight of divorcées, they argue, who suddenly find themselves having to support six or seven kids. "Some mothers have no training," commented one studio teacher.[2] "Their only option is to go to work as secretaries. This means they're gone from the home, leaving the children with no supervision after school, holed up all alone in a shabby apartment." There are many others in the business, however, who believe that mothers who allow themselves to be supported by their children are more likely to be motivated by their own needs than their children's. Says a disdainful Norman Lear, "I am sure some parents use the child to earn more money than they know they could earn themselves."

It is the rare Hollywood parent who imbues the child with a sense of proportion when it comes to money. "Nothing was ever given to me," says an appreciative Jane Withers today. "Mama made sure that, whether I was making five or ten thousand dollars a week, I got an allowance that I had to work for. I had to make my bed and clean my room, even though we had five live-in helpers." Sonda Peluce, mother of ten-year-old Meeno Peluce (*Best of the West*, 1981–1982; *Voyagers!* 1982–), believes "a child should know what his worth is." Her son meets regularly with his accountant, she says, and "is aware of what he has down to the penny."

[2]The Los Angeles Unified School District certifies and assigns studio teacher-child labor representatives.

With or without a parent's financial tutelage, however, before long most child actors spot the dollar signs flashing across their parents' eyes the way other kids figure out how to master video games. My parents bought me stocks, but today Hollywood parents tend to go in for houses and condominiums. Successful child actors can look forward to such gifts as horses, delivered with bows tied around their necks, for Christmas. "It would be great if I could have a ranch," says eleven-year-old Sydney Penny. "But instead, I might save and just have a horse and stables." Linda Blair vividly recalls a telling series of conversations with her mother. "I loved horses when I was little," she explains, "but my mother said, 'We cannot afford to give them to you. If you work and save your money, then you get what you want.' " Linda had already gotten plenty. At the age of five, embarked on a highly successful modeling career, she was featured in Sears, Roebuck catalogues and TV commercials. But as she got older, she became less interested in acting and more interested in horses. With perfect timing, her mother played the one card that would keep Linda interested in show business. "I never knew I could act. I wanted to be a veteri-narian when I was little. If I had been raised with money, I would have gone on and just worked with horses. But acting supported that [the horses]." Years later, in her early twenties, she attempted to revitalize her sagging career by posing nude for *Oui* magazine. Her mother was appalled, but Linda de-fended herself well; she reminded her mother that it was not fair to condemn her for resorting to any means to survive in the business that *she herself* had put her little girl into at the age of five.

Child actors are taught early to appreciate the rewards of stardom. At a commercial workshop one Saturday morning in Hollywood, the casting director advised some forty preteen students, "If on the set they switch lines so that most of yours are taken away and the other kid gets them, don't get upset and cry. You'll get the same amount of money. I said nothing on an M and M commercial and I got twenty thousand dollars." Says Jerry Mathers, "When I was two and a half, I started to want a German shepherd. I pushed my parents to land me some modeling jobs to get the shepherd." One day, when he and his mother were strolling through a department store in Los Angeles, a store administrator stopped them to remark pleasantly that Jerry looked almost exactly like the little boy in the family of models the store had been using for this year's Christmas ad campaign. Trouble was, said the official, the little two year old had already outgrown his winter clothes. Rather than hire an entirely new family, he proposed to "adopt" Jerry as the store's new model son. From there, his career took off. He attracted the eye of Hollywood print photographers and became a topnotch model. One day, he remembers his parents saying, "We can only afford a small dog, but if you make the money you can have a big one.' Then my agent called and said, 'They want you for a TV show.' So there was my German Shepherd." I got the impression that Jerry's ambitions soon extended to running a kennel. Surely one *Leave It to Beaver* episode provided enough to buy Lassie.

"We delighted in that make-believe world," Mickey Rooney told me, "and we were paid well."

Besides the money in Hollywood, mothers love the glamour. Cecile Provost, mother of Jon Provost (Timmy Martin on *Lassie*, 1957–1964), recalls that her love affair with show business originated when she was teaching Sunday school. One morning a fellow teacher asked her if she had read Hedda Hopper's Sunday column in the *Los Angeles Times* about the search for a little boy to play Jane Wyman's infant son in the Warner Brothers movie *So Big* (1953). " 'I don't know any little actors,' " Cecile remembers innocently replying. "The teacher said, 'They don't expect them to act.' She said Jon was so sweet he was a natural. My husband argued with me. He said the item in Hopper's column was a publicity stunt. I said, 'I don't care—I want to see Jane Wyman.' "

She took little Jon to the open call. The casting office at Warners was in turmoil. There were about three hundred kids there, every one of whom seemed to be crying and screaming for food. At least two hundred were crawling underneath chairs. Despite the human anthill of competition, the Sunday school teacher's hunch proved correct. Distinguishing himself with quiet manners and obedient responses to the casting director's instructions, Jon won the part, and Cecile got to see Jane Wyman on the *So Big* set.

Accidents like these do not happen to unambitious mothers. At the heart of any child actor's success story lies the force of a mother's will to succeed. Take the story of the aspiring young actress and model who went on a call for a modeling job, and took her breast-feeding child along. *She* didn't get the job, but her *daughter* did. At nine and a half pounds, her cherubic looking little girl turned out to be the perfect size for the line of infant clothing the client was also aiming to illustrate in the advertising brochure. Was the baby really at the interview, as her mother insists, because she couldn't land a sitter? Or because she was secretly hoping her daughter would land a job, even if she didn't? In truth, when the opportunity beckoned, she exhibited scant resistance. "The business can only enhance someone's childhood," she told me, "in terms of social interaction and learning discipline. . . . And with my background in acting, it's wonderful that my daughter has me." This is the usual kind of self-justification among stage parents. Fledgling actors and actresses commonly bring offspring to their own auditions. "After all, *someone* might see her," one struggling male actor said of his eight-month-old baby. "It has happened that way before." Yes, it has.

Musically speaking, the ability to perform in front of an audience was a long-standing tradition on my mother's side of the family. Around 1905 my grandparents fled the persecution of the Jews by the Russian Cossacks in Odessa, emigrated to America, settled into New York City's Lower East Side and raised a family of three. My grandmother supplemented her income as a factory seamstress by teaching piano for twenty-five cents a lesson.

My grandmother always had a tremendous passion for

music, and taught the piano to her daughter Evelyn at a very early age. At six years old, Evelyn began formal piano study at New York City's famous Third Street Music School Settlement; she continued her training over a period of twenty years. "I wasn't studying regularly all that time," she always told me as I grew up, "because I knew I wasn't going to be a great concert pianist. It's a solo instrument. You have to be tops, or there's no room for you. You have to be a superstar."

Nonetheless, my mother did enjoy some early moments in the spotlight. Obsessed with the idea of forming a family trio, Evelyn's mother started one son on the cello, the other on the violin. The three played together wherever the Third Street Music School Settlement could arrange concert performances, whether at Town Hall, or in an auditorium at Ellis Island for a government-financed show. Individual spot bookings began to come the boys' way. In his twenties, Evelyn's younger brother became assistant concertmaster of the Pittsburgh Symphony under Fritz Reiner. The older cellist played in the NBC Symphony under Toscanini.

Success such as this was harder for my mother to come by. She soon came to understand that the piano was an impractical instrument, on which she would never be able to build a concert career. No great concern: boys grew up to have careers; girls grew up to be married and have children. When she was twenty-five years old, the Depression hit, and the family scraped by with the help of the income her piano lessons provided. With the advent of World War II, my mother's life changed dramatically. She married; her husband was drafted into the army on their first anniversary. Dutifully, she followed him across the country to wherever he happened to be stationed. She played the piano at big-time events in small towns across the country like Chandler, Arizona, but the piano was more a form of psychic therapy than a serious professional venture. When a town weekly would write her up as a big-time concert pianist visiting from New York City, she would be profoundly amused, sometimes embarrassed.

When the war was over and she began to raise a family,

my mother continued to teach the piano, but with less interest. Childrearing became her full-time career. "I was so crazy about the kids; *that* was fulfillment," she told me many years later. "I didn't need another career."

"I figured my son might be an actor because at eighteen months, I caught him making faces in the mirror," says Barrie Howard, chair of the Screen Actors Guild Children's Committee. "When he was three, I knew they were looking for a young John Travolta for the ABC-TV movie *The Boy in the Plastic Bubble* (1976). I heard rumors they needed a kid with dark hair and blue eyes— and who wouldn't be afraid of being confined. But when I got pregnant again, I said I was quitting him in the business. My son cried and screamed. He said, 'Don't stop me, I love it!' " Her son Seth seconds the account, "I told her I'd be real good. No matter what happens, I always want to act." Only the boy's persistence, his mother says, kept him in the business. Only *his own* ambition, and talent, got him started.

Maybe, but knowledgeable people in the entertainment industry understandably tend to be skeptical. *"No way* can a child of seven say, 'Mother, Dad, this is what I want to do,' " says former child star Peggy Ann Garner, "he doesn't have the intelligence to know what it involves." Says producer Joel Rogosin (*Ironside, Mr. Merlin, Magnum, P.I.*), "I always have the impression it's the mother's initiative."

Children are highly susceptible to parental indoctrination. "At a very early age, acting is just play," I was told by author Diana Serra Cary, formerly Baby Peggy, child star of silent movies such as *Playmates* (1920) and *The Kid Reporter* (1921), "Mothers immediately parlay that into a career." Her comment reminded me of how my mother, and eventually I, viewed the launching of my career. Whenever I asked her why she put me into show business, she would proceed to explain that I seemed inclined to the performing arts almost at birth, as if I plied out of her womb in ballet shoes. She'd recall my initial performance at nursery school, belting out "Love and marriage, love and marriage/ Go together like a horse and carriage." Or how, the first time they took me to a dance hall and the sound of live music punctured my baby brain, I erupted into rapturous dancing—still wearing diapers.

Mine is a familiar tale, like so many others. "My favorite story," one vocal coach told me, "is this one. A mother came to the audition for my showcase with a baby in a stroller. The baby was not yet three. She could barely talk, and was drooling. I said, 'Who are you auditioning?' She said it was the baby in the stroller, but I couldn't believe it. The baby cried. So her mother picked her up, put her on the stage, held the microphone, and, incredibly, she sang a little bit of 'Tomorrow'. I told the mother her baby was great, but she was a little young. I wanted that kid out of my life, at least for a year or two. She had a vocabulary limited to, 'Mommy, I'm hungry.' But her mother said, 'I wouldn't be here if it weren't that she wants this business.' "

Parents readily project adult drives onto their toddlers. When six-year-old Darryl Hickman asked his mother why he was an actor, she replied, "It's something you've always wanted to do." Says Hickman, "I started when I was three. Yet she kept telling me how I was *born* to do that." In extreme cases, the child's career would appear to have been born even before the child. The mother of one four-year-old girl whom I interviewed after she appeared in an amateur showcase in Los Angeles ("The Too Short for Prime Time Players") literally nurtured the embryo of her little girl's dream. "When she was in my stomach and music was on, I could feel her moving around," her mother told me, dead serious. "While *I* have no musical abilities, I knew then that she was self-motivated."

A mother's rationale for getting her child started in the business is often the direct opposite of that which she uses to keep her career going. The mother of a successful child will lie about his age, lengthen scores of hems, and do anything she can to retain the lucrative virtues of her child's youth. At the *outset* of her child's career, however, she may boast about how intelligent, mature, ambitious and determined he is, portraying him as a miniature adult, even though the idea was hers, of course, not her child's. "She doesn't fight me about going to bed early the night before an audition. For anything else she might, but not for a job," says the mother of a four-year-old aspiring actress, painting a picture of determination that rattles credulity.

When famous child actor Tommy Rettig (Jeff Miller on *Lassie*, 1954–1957) hit the road at the age of five with a Joshua Logan production of the musical *Annie Get Your Gun*, starring Mary Martin, his parents saw the opportunity as a ticket to escape an economic prison. "It was 1942, and my Dad worked in a defense plant," Rettig recalls. "I remember my Mom sitting by a night light sewing with this old clankety-clank machine that you ran by foot. My mother had worked at a department store as a junior executive but was taking in sewing to be home with me. Then, fifty cents meant a lot. So the fifty-five dollars a week I started at . . . well, I was making more than my Dad. And all of a sudden I had the potential of being not just another schnook in Jackson Heights on the streets of New York.

"Given the choice of going to school in New York or traveling and seeing the country with the road company, I chose the latter. But then my parents said, 'Only one of us can go with you for financial reasons.' So I changed my mind and said, 'I don't want to go.' I didn't want to break up the family, which is perfectly normal for any five year old. Then I was told that we were *all* going to go. So we packed and got on the train at Grand Central Station. Just before the train literally pulled out, my Dad jumped off. My mother copped to it right away. She said, 'You wouldn't have done this otherwise. We both really want you to do it. It's for you and your own good, and you're going to love this.' I cried . . ."

Mothers put their children on the fast track to Hollywood as soon as they can; whether the children want to climb aboard is of minor concern. "I just kind of grew up in the business," says Kristy McNichol, whose mother, then a Hollywood extra, first got the idea of putting her two cute, all-American-looking kids (Kristy and brother, actor Jimmy McNichol) into show business when Kristy was eight. "I wasn't against it. When I got to be eighteen is when I started making some decisions by myself, not before that."

An altogether different matter is the child who starts his career later, perhaps as late as eleven or twelve. At that age, reasonably thoughtful decisions *can* be made. Well aware of the money at stake, especially compared to the alternative of working for slave wages in a fast food joint or department store, the child can hardly be blamed for wanting to go to Hollywood. One ambitious eleven-year-old girl described how she had to overcome a degree of initial opposition from her mother in order to get her career going. She took it upon herself to arrange for the publicity photo session, and to see that the pictures were sent around the agents' circuit. When she got her first call expressing interest, she told her mother nothing but simply hopped on a Los Angeles bus to confer with her agent. Only when a call for an audition finally came through did she inform her mother of what she had been up to; she desperately needed her mother to give her a ride to the audition. No one makes it anywhere on time relying on the bus system of Los Angeles. "Her mother was a little upset," recalls Screen Actors Guild Children's Committee chair Barrie Howard, "but she got the job." Thanks to her mother, who got her there on time.

My mother determined to give her kids the best she could. That meant dancing lessons for my sister at the American School of Ballet on Hollywood Boulevard, located in what was then a building known as the Garden Court Apartments just a half block west of the famous Grauman's Chinese Theater. In its heyday, its tenants included Louis B. Mayer, John Barrymore, Stan Laurel and Oliver Hardy. I used to tag along after my sister; I loved this huge, dark, impressive building and delighted in watching the older kids dance. As the mothers intently followed their daughters' balletic progress from week to week, I'd peer through the glass doors of the studio and shout to anyone who would listen, "I've waited all my life to dance!" At the age of five, however, I was still a bit young to attract Balanchine's attention!

As the weeks and months went by, one of the mothers, who worked as a Hollywood extra and whose daughter in the class had done both films and commercials, took notice of this endlessly talkative and aggressive Andrea. When she suggested that I be taken to an agent, my mother was skeptical. As if wanting to prove that she knew a moneymaker when she saw one, the friend marched over to a pay phone and made an appointment for us with her agent. My mother's resistance crumbled. "I didn't know what to make of it," she says today. "I knew you were a child with musical talent. What did I have to lose?" My father was positively enthusiastic. A research librarian at Universal Studios for many years, he was unabashedly fascinated by Hollywood. "I *did* think of it in the future sense, the sense of someday becoming an important person," he told me not long ago. When the idea first struck, he in fact approached a casting director at Universal about finding me some work. He got the standard reply: "Find an agent."

My sister came with us to see the agent. We were both accepted as clients, but I know now that she stood virtually no chance of picking up work. She was approaching the age of thirteen, the most awkward period for any child actor or actress. But the agent, having nothing to lose by the acquisitions, took us both.

A year passed, I turned seven, but the agent never called. Then one day, when she telephoned to remind us that we needed to update our pictures for her client book, my mother responded sharply that nothing had come of the initial investment last year and that it seemed silly to order a new round of photographs for no good reason. But the agent was a pro. "She kind of talked me into it," my mother remembers. New pictures were ordered up.

A few months later, I got my first "break." One afternoon the agent telephoned my mother, who picked me up at school and frantically rushed me over to Desilu Studios in Hollywood. They needed a little girl who could sing to appear in an episode of the weekly TV dramatic series *Desilu Playhouse* (1958–1960). John Green, the Academy Award-winning conductor, composer, and arranger of such films as *An American in Paris* (1945) and *Oliver* (1968), was making his debut as a television conductor in a musical episode starring Robert Strauss and Anna Maria Alberghetti. When we got to the studio, we realized the reason for the rush. The little girl whom they had originally chosen for the singing role had suddenly, and inexplicably, refused to open her mouth. A panicky search for a replacement was quickly ordered.

This was my chance to prove to myself, and to my mother, that I could do it. My mother briskly took her place at the piano and pounded out a song we rehearsed at home from the musical *South Pacific*. I sang like I had never sung before—with polish, relish and punch. When I was finished, there was a brief silence. Then John Green picked me up in his arms, hugged and kissed me, put me on his shoulder and asked if he could take me home. When I said "Yes," they both laughed. My mother left the studio that afternoon with me under one arm and my first television script and musical score tucked under the other. At the age of seven, I had won my first role: a singing-and-acting part playing the South American daughter of actor Robert Strauss in *Desilu Playhouse's* opening show of the 1959 season, *A Diamond for Carla*.

"A stage mother is one who doesn't know she's one," says Hollywood photographer Buddy Rosenberg. Stage mothers *are* remarkable specimens. In interview after interview for this book, I continually found myself wondering: How can she be so blind? So blunt? So contradictory?

"I'm *not* a yenta," one stage mother told me, "but if you're in the business, you have to do it all the way. My children have to *want* to do a project, unless of course I feel it's right on the mark for them . . . Sometimes I feel guilty. I know I'm denying them their games and sports. But that's what *they're* choosing, I guess."

The persuasive mother convinces herself with her own deceptive line. "The thing that surprises me the most about this business," says Hollywood agent Evelyn Schultz, "is how initially sweet, unaggressive, nice mothers, after a little success, suddenly become barracudas. All of a sudden their kids are absolute *stars*, and they're not making enough money, not getting enough interviews, not getting the jobs they want their kids to get. Two years ago they were excited just to get an interview, now they've got delusions of grandeur."

"They become nervous wrecks," says agent Don Schwartz. "Once they get into it they ruin the child . . . by changing agents; or talking in front of the child about money, jobs; or why he isn't working more. . . . Stage mothers should quit trying to think of careers. They should think of the kid's enjoyment." In Hollywood, the image is universal. On your average set, no matter how unobtrusively they slink around, the mothers are inevitably regarded as potential setbacks to the production schedule. "We know we're regarded as necessary evils," says Vivian Hollander, mother of twelve-year-old David Hollander (the ABC-TV movie *Whale for the Killing*, 1981; *Scavenger Hunt*, 1979). "But you can't be intimidated by an image that follows you wherever you go. Directors talk to the teachers, but not the mothers. Often the mothers are asked to leave the scene of the shooting, even if they've done nothing wrong."

Stage mothers have their own concerns. Some of them may even be well-founded; all of them provide grist for the famous Mothers' Underground mill. Also known as the Mothers' Grapevine, this is the informal, virtually twenty-four-hour telephone hotline over which the fastest, latest-breaking news is transmitted about: (1) the hottest, and coldest, agents; (2) which child was last interviewed for which job, and (3) whose child is getting over the hill (i.e., becoming a teenager). The Mothers' Grapevine, a most lethal stage mother perversion, can produce utterly irrational verbal assaults upon innocent agents, managers, even rival children and their parents.

The Mothers' Grapevine has many branches: mothers of old-timers; mothers of newcomers; mothers of the hottest kids; mothers of the fading kids; mothers of toddlers; mothers of children in their prime (ages six to ten); mothers of black children; mothers of Hispanics. Favored face-to-face meeting sites for any of those branches are the pediatric/cosmetic/dentist's office near Hollywood and the casting offices. "It's an *after-the-fact* information service," explains former long-time children's agent Dorothy Day Otis. "They say things like, 'I was on a Kellogg's commercial interview with my child. Why weren't *you* there? All the other kids *like yours* were.' "

Of course! No Hollywood mother in her right mind would risk telling the parent of a rival child about a part that was available. Unlike a suicide prevention service or a venereal disease hotline, there is nothing preventive about the Mothers' Grapevine. "The talk is vicious," agrees agent Evelyn Schultz. "I got a letter from a mother the other day: 'Dear Evelyn, I think you should know that one of your clients [and she named the client] takes her daughter to interviews that she's heard about from other mothers, even though she's not supposed to be on that interview. Signed, Anonymous.' Then there was the mother of one little boy who did twenty-four commercials in one year. She told me she used to get anonymous phone calls saying, 'This is one job your child didn't get.' Click!"

My mother grew to loathe the Grapevine. "They drove me crazy," she says. "They were like a beehive. I didn't like it, but I got caught up in it. They were *all* caught up in it, like a vicious circle. They'd say, 'Were you out on such and such interview? You weren't! Andrea was exactly what they were looking for!' They *forced* me to do things. I started to feel that maybe the agents weren't doing their best for you. I felt obligated to act on what they said, as if I wasn't doing right by my child if I didn't listen to them."

Hollywood agent Doris Ross of Associated Talent first discovered the Mothers' Grapevine syndrome, with all its prickly extensions, when she took her five-year-old daughter to a jam-packed casting call. "I noticed the kids seemed to stumble when they walked into the room to be interviewed," she says. "At first, I thought they were just clumsy. Then I thought, 'What is going on here?' Finally, I saw that there was one mother who was sitting by the door with her legs crossed, and as some of the kids went in, she'd move her foot to trip them. Now, if a child is on an interview, he will be a little nervous to begin with. Half of them would start crying, and you knew they'd go in and blow the interview. This mother had identified the new kids who were not in her little clique and picked them off one by one with her foot."

Mothers in Hollywood tend to feel that they are in the front lines of that Hollywood combat zone fighting not just for their children, but for their very own lives. "Stage mothers make demands on you as if they believe *they themselves* are doing the [acting] work," says agent Don Schwartz.

"It's one thing to be a prideful parent. It's another to be a parent who *identifies* with his kid," says Dr. Michael Mantell, former chief psychologist of Children's Hospital in San Diego. "If a mother sits in the audience and sees herself dancing when the kid dances, she is living vicariously. There is a clinical term, 'projective identification.' You take on the identity of another person. When someone else's identity is in you, you lose your own. Some of these kids probably feel engulfed, devoured by their mothers."

"Even now, she refuses to let go," a famous former child actress says of her mother. "She always wanted to do something with her life. She had the brains and ambition, but lacked the talent. I *didn't* have the drive or the ambition, but I *had* the talent."

The child/mother relationship that flourishes in the entertainment world can be devastatingly symbiotic. The child wants to get the part to please his mother. Then the mother becomes more excited than the child. When the child doesn't get the job, he gets nervous, and so does his mother. At this point, she either punishes or overindulges him. The two feed off of one another, and every exchange of emotions snowballs uncontrollably.

"I see this kind of thing every day," says Dr. Mantell. "Mothers who push their kids to have a thousand friends. But the nature of the entertainment business is different, because of the economic factor. In few other things can a child earn money with which to support the family. And to put the child into *that* level of fame is a different matter."

Stage mothers may be of either sex, of course. Men can be just as anxious to make their children stars. The predominance of female stage parents to date is a product of historical circumstance. It has always been more routine for women to make their children the central focus of their lives; it is easier for them to wrap their vicarious needs and personal ambitions in the socially acceptable cloak of concerned motherhood. But in the liberated environment of the eighties, not to skirt the issue, more and more men are getting into the act. And as the magnitude of the fortune the child star may reap continues to grow, so may a commitment to a venture that makes increasing economic sense.

The stage father can display all the offensive traits of his female counterpart. Indeed, Hollywood managers and agents tend to find today's male stage mother as difficult to deal with as his historical predecessor. In fact, he is one of the least acclaimed byproducts of the liberation of the sexes. In this respect, at least, I was most fortunate. In the early sixties, men had not yet broadened their horizons. There *were* no stage fathers, thank God.

Like the female trailblazers in the field of stage parenting, fathers will abandon their careers for the sake of their children. Dolores Jacoby's husband, for example, was originally a freelance building contractor before his wife persuaded him to give up his business to take several of their children on tour with a Joshua Logan road show of *Rip Van Winkle*. Now the Jacobys in effect function as co-managers of their very successful children. "He is so accommodating," says Dolores of her husband, who now works as a set designer. "He just won't call in for work if I need him to take one of the kids on location for a job, or if I have a conflict, like three kids working in one day. At first he said to me, 'What are you exposing them to?' But then he saw the fun. Now he's all for it."

To fathers who find the entertainment industry appealing, participating in their children's careers is hardly a sacrifice.

Harry Gold, himself a former actor and the father of Missy (*Benson*), Tracey (*Shoot the Moon*, 1982) and Brandy (*Baby Makes Five*, 1983), was ecstatic when the director of a commercial rejected him but after taking one look at Tracey said, "That's the kid I want for this commercial." Sitting on sets with either of the three was no source of discomfort: "Being an actor, I wasn't working all the time," Gold recalls. "My wife, who wasn't working then, shared the responsibilities. I was always involved in the filmmaking process and I liked being there with my children." He is now running Harry Gold and Associates, an actors' agency representing both children and adults. Missy, Tracey and Brandy are among his clients. "They love it," he says. "Why wouldn't they want to have their father be their agent? I have had all three in series. I think it's great!"

A father's place is not ordinarily in the home. When traditional roles are reversed, stage fathers, not having those office jobs, tend to develop intense insecurities that lead to a compensatory overassertiveness and ruthlessness. Insists one manager, "Fathers are more dominant and possessive of the child. A mother may *think* about her son or daughter becoming a star, but a father is more verbal. He wants to show that he's a man, and that no one's taking advantage of him."

To Margaret O'Brien it was a desperate father who stands out most vividly among the overly ambitious characters she met in Hollywood. "There was another little girl who was very close to getting *Journey for Margaret*, she remembers. "In fact, some people were leaning more towards her than me. But I happened to get it. That father practically ended up in a mental institution over that child's career. He worked as an electrician for the studio. One time, he tried to drop a light on me." He missed. He made his point, but Margaret O'Brien completed the film that catapulted her into stardom.

Jay North was escorted to the first interview for *Dennis the Menace* (1959–1963), by his uncle, who was not the kind of man to give up easily. "The first time, I gave a terrible reading," Jay told me. "A few weeks later, my uncle brought me back (on the sly) and asked a secretary for a script. He brought it home and read the scene over with me. He convinced the agent, who convinced the casting director, to let me go back. So then I was tested." Thanks to his uncle's fierce male ego, Jay North got to be The Menace.

Push comes to shove in the home. With the Division of Labor Standards Enforcement hovering in the background monitoring grades, ready to revoke work permits for failing students, a mother may have to apply heavy pressure on her schoolchildren. At the same time as they are trying to please their teachers, show business children must placate other masters. "You *always* have to go to the interview. You can't cancel because of a sleepover party," says eleven-year-old Jennifer Horton (CBS TV's *Not in Front of the Children*, 1982). "You know that to be a movie star, you can't have everything you want. You've got to suffer. I've always felt that way, but my mother says that too."

The mother's presence is everywhere. On interviews, there is more to the mother's role than chauffering the child to the casting office and waiting idly outside; a mother must double as her child's dialogue coach. "If there's a script, I always make sure to park the car early and go with my kids to look at it," says one. "We interpret what kind of a kid they want. I don't just throw them to the dogs." Says twelve-year-old Shane Butterworth, whose mother is also his personal manager, "She gets me all hyper before going in. She makes me laugh, tickles me, patts my butt and says, 'Do your best, be on your toes, be talkative, be bright as a lightbulb.' " Mothers of nervous children employ different techniques. "I try to give her a quiet morning," says the mother of four-year-old Hayley Taylor, "and keep her as natural as I can."

After the interview, a mother expects her reward, a point-by-point playback of everything that transpired behind that closed door. "I want to prepare my kids in case there's a callback," says one. "But the kids don't always want to tell me. They will talk only if they're in good moods. I say, 'I bothered to pick you up and take you to the call, give me my bread-crumb!' "

When the casting decision is rendered on the spot (a common procedure for a small part) the child may be faced with instant retribution for not landing the job. Casting executive Eve Brandstein (*One Day at a Time, Square Pegs, The Facts of Life,* etc.) remembers interviewing for a television episode one girl who had been severely threatened by her mother before going in. "I sensed there was a high degree of poverty in the family, and her mother knew this could mean easy money," says Brandstein. "As the kid walked in for the interview, I heard her mother say something like, 'I know you will mess it up, so don't. You know what will happen if you do!' The kid sat in my office frozen. She couldn't speak. There was such terror on her face! At best, she read her lines deadpan and uninspiringly." When the girl finished her flat reading, Brandstein decided to try to deceive the mother so as to spare the child the rod. "I tried to make her mother think it was a terrific reading," says Brandstein. But when she led the girl by the hand back to her mother, "the fear was still on the child's face. It was obvious how the interview had really gone. The mother dragged her by the arm to the elevator and I heard her say, 'No dinner for you tonight!' " The girl was only eight years old.

The hard-core stage mother's behavior may indeed border on child abuse. During my own career, I worked with an adorable little tow-headed boy whose mother was prepared to risk almost anything for success. She habitually fed her son unnutritious food for lunch, in tiny portions, whether a piece of bread, or a few leaves of lettuce, while everyone else on the set wolfed down a hearty lunch at the Farmer's Market across the street from CBS. The mother apparently was acting on the belief that the less he was fed, the less he would grow. By stunting his growth, she would in effect lengthen his career as a child actor. The Mothers' Grapevine caught on to the story. So had an irate flock of studio teachers. But with no bruises on his wrists or scars on his face, there were no tell-tale signs of classic child abuse to interest the district attorney's office.

Even today, some Hollywood children have parents who enforce a very special diet. "This little girl would come to the studio school and say, 'I'm hungry,' " says Margaret Doughty, business representative of the studio teachers' union. "Or she would come in, spot a box of donuts set out for the adults, grab half a donut and start eating. Then her mother learned to look to see where the child was in proximity to the donuts on the set." This little girl's dreams are not about landing a major dramatic role, but a part in a breakfast or dinner scene with real food on the table! Once, when she was filming a scene set in a dining room and her mother happened to be away from the set, real waffles were put on the table for the dress rehearsal. While the other children toyed uninterestedly with the food as they delivered their lines, she scarfed down the first stack of waffles in minutes. When the mother returned to the set to discover her daughter's transgression, she began pillorying the teacher for not restraining the girl's appetite. This child, now notorious in Hollywood circles, attracts sympathy wherever she goes. "If there's food in the room, you can't direct her, but you *can* feed her," says casting director Sheila Manning. "When she was little, she was afraid to take food. Now, I take her into a room and give her junk food. Ironically, she's gotten several roles as an abused child."

Even when they are observed, laws protecting child actors are not always adequate. New York child labor regulations are notoriously lax (see Chapter Five). Situations in which children are abused are legally forbidden (although not always in reality deterred) by California law. But where the state may be protective, the parent may not. "I have never seen a parent keep a child at home sick," remarks one veteran studio teacher. "It's a terrible quandary for the parent. When the child has gotten a part, here's this company with everyone waiting. Do they call and put X thousands of dollars down the tube, or do they take a chance and hope the child can get through the day's work?"

The choice involves more than immediate priorities for the parent. In Hollywood, the child's reputation for reliability can be severely damaged when he fails to show up on the set. "If the parents are just starting the child," explains one studio teacher, "they are worried about getting blacklisted." The children share the worry. They know that on every job it is important to excel. Should they forget what is at stake, chances are their agents will remind them. When, for example, fourteen-year-old Susan Page, who was allergic to bees, had the bad luck to be stung by one at the beach on a Sunday, her mother called her agent on Monday to cancel out of her Wednesday shoot. But as it was a good-paying, topnotch job (a toothpaste commercial), the agent was insistent. "If it takes a wheelchair, *go*," she advised. Recalls Susan, "My foot was swollen huge. They all knew about the bee sting. When I told them I'd have to wear a bedroom slipper on one foot, they said they'd only shoot from the waist up. I was limping, it hurt so much. They did sixty-seven takes just for one shot." With a reputation for such show-must-go-on tenacity, the girl, now a proven pro, has more than 100 commercial assignments in the bank. Word quickly gets around Hollywood. "There is one director who said he will only work with a couple of kids," Susan's mother, children's manager Jean Page, told me, brimming with pride. "He calls them his silver bullets. Susan is one of them because she never complains."

In almost any other line of work, a sick employee will be sent home. Not the child actor. During my own career, illnesses took a back seat to ambition. "I don't know *why* I did it," my mother admitted to me, thinking back some twenty years to the time when, despite my suffering from a ferocious viral infection, she kept me working on an episode of *The Danny Thomas Show* (1953–1971). After the first day of rehearsal, when the studio teacher–child labor representative expressed concern about my well-being, my mother rushed me to the emergency ward of the local hospital clinic. At my mother's behest, the doctor on duty signed a note attesting to the fact that while I was sick (my temperature was *only* in the low hundreds), I could still work. (Maybe looking at the two of us, he realized that if I lost the job, my mother would become ill!) The next morning, doctor's note in hand, she escorted me back to the set. Before every set of lines, and during every break, she ladled spoonfuls of cough medicine down my small eleven-year-old throat to drown out the coughing attacks. As she put it, "At that time, there were few parts for you and you were getting a lot of publicity about the *Danny Thomas* role. God forbid someone else should do the part! Today it means nothing, and I felt a lot of guilt about it afterwards. It was a stupid, terrible thing to do and I admit it."

In the long run, perhaps, excessive cruelty will mother a negative reputation. No one wants to tangle with a pushy mom; it may be easier to hire another child. Word of the nasty mother tends to travel as fast as the rave review.

Some interviewers will even attempt a rough assessment of the character of the mother before casting the child. New York vocal coach Robert Marks, who runs a showcase for children in New York, has a rating system that also grades the mothers. When he writes his remarks on the backs of photos and résumés of children at an audition, he will sometimes make the following notation in bold red ink capital letters: SM, for Stage Mother. SM is definitely no compliment; the child with such a notation on his record will not be cast. Marks believes that no child can be so talented as to make up for an obnoxious mother. Paramount Studios casting director Bobby Hoffman conceded to me that before concluding an interview with a child actor he makes it a habit to wander into his outer offices just to spy on the mother. "I pretend to be going out to see my secretary," he says. If Hoffman is having difficulty deciding between two kids, the one whose mother appears likely to be a real troublemaker will not get the job. It is a wise insurance policy. "There have been cases where they've said they would never hire a child again because of the parent," says former Disney Studios casting director Pam Polifroni. "Some of them are unbelievable. They place constant demands for special things—a greater amount of expense money, or sending the limousine to take the kid to work and then wanting it to stop along the way, so the mother can shop. You try to deal diplomatically, but sometimes you just say 'No.' "

Photographs help round out the picture of how far some mothers are prepared to go. "I *have* had mothers come in who want to exploit their daughters," says Hollywood photographer Margo Vann. "They say, 'Look what a body she has, maybe she can get some sexy parts.' They'd love it if I'd take a nude shot. But I try to discourage that, telling the mothers to be careful because once the kid is in that area, she's typecast." Better to be typecast than *not* cast! "A lot of mothers want their daughters to look like Brooke Shields," says Los Angeles photographer Buddy Rosenberg. "They want a twelve year old to look twenty and wear low-cut blouses. Then I say, 'I'll do it, if it's okay by her manager and agent.' But you do not shoot a thirteen year old looking eighteen, unless there's a reason for it. The agent usually says she needs a certain look—older, okay, but not like Brooke Shields."

After a certain age, there is little room for innocence in Hollywood, of course. Once my mother mailed some new photographs that had been taken of me to one of my favorite directors. At the age of sixteen, a washed-out child actress, what chance did I have of getting work? Only a director who had adored me when I was younger would bother trying to convince a producer to hire me. If some glamourous publicity stills succeeded in reminding him that I existed, why not send them?

But the director's response to the pictures was not what I wanted. Telephoning me at my parents' house, he began his thrust-and-parry with, "What are your measurements?" While I had grown accustomed to directors asking me for my height in inches, questions about the specifics of my chest and hips marked a turning point in my career. Still, a sixteen year old determined not to seem like a child anymore, I answered every question.

"Has *it* happened yet?"

"Has what happened?" I replied, truly not knowing what he meant.

"If you have to ask, the answer's 'No,' " he said, laughing.

Feeling humiliated and demeaned, but also desperately wanting to work again, I tried to affect an air of cool sophistication. When he invited me to come swimming at his house, I said that would be fine.

Only my mother's intervention put a stop to it before the matter got out of hand. "I'm sorry, but as long as she's under my jurisdiction she doesn't have permission to go," she told him. "I didn't mean any harm by it," he replied. He truly may have been shocked. Surely he'd been approached before with much more daring pictures submitted by much more daring mothers.

Were we wrong about his intentions? Did we jeopardize my chances for a comeback? Three years later, when I was home from college one Christmas, he called again. I was nineteen and for the first time on my own. Planning on being home for the summer, I was still hopeful of picking up some acting work. This time, his telephone manners were more reserved. He invited me to his home in the Hollywood Hills. I accepted. What could my mother say? I was over eighteen.

Soon after I got there, I realized that the scene he had in mind for me was not about a come*back*, but a come-on. When I arrived the door was slightly open, and through an intercom he invited me in to wait while he finished showering. "You grew a nice pair of tits while I was away," he said, shouting down to me from the top of the stairs, towel strategically wrapped around him. He then flung a string of deeply intimate and incredibly perverse questions at me. I will spare you the obvious, but when he pulled me to the floor and whispered definite somethings in my ear, offering to direct me in a way no director had done before, I pushed him away and bolted out of his house. As I drove home, I realized how lucky I was to have had a mother who shielded me from command performances like this when I was younger.

The phrase "it all depends upon the parents,"—commonly used by directors, agents and producers to disclaim any direct moral responsibility for the potentially negative long-range psychic effect of career pressures on the child—resounds throughout Hollywood with the ringing sincerity of "the check is in the mail."

Very special parents, in any field, can successfully trot a

child over the trickiest territory. "Parents can act as a bridge between the glitter and the rest of the world," says Manhattan-based child psychiatrist Richard Atkins. "But it takes an exceptional parent to do that." Most parents are clearly not exceptional. Says Sonda Peluce, mother of child actor Meeno Peluce, "A lot of children don't want to do it and the parents push them. I have stepped in sometimes and told them, 'Listen to your child.' Then they say, 'What do they know, they're just kids.' "

Parents who are trying to raise their children conscientiously will insist on subordinating the demands of the industry to the welfare of the child. Prudent parents are careful to establish the rule that acting is only one element of their children's lives. Priorities are established on the basis of the children's needs and feelings, not the parents' ambitions. "Meeno was offered a real good TV *Movie of the Week* at the same time as a part in *Amityville Horror* [1979]," says Sonda Peluce. "He was more excited about doing a horror film, but it was a lesser role. I supported his decision."

One properly cautious and responsible parent can rein in another. One morning at Los Angeles International Airport, ex-Mouseketeer Bobby Burgess ran into an old colleague named Mary Grady, one of his former agents. Bursting with fatherly pride, he pulled out a picture of his then two-year-old daughter Becky from his wallet. Grady, of course, had to say the baby was gorgeous, adding that if he was interested, she would try her hand at selling her. Bobby wasted no time at all. Within days, he had a composite of the baby ordered up, and Becky soon started to pick up work as a model for print ads.

One of Becky's first TV commercial calls did not end as planned. "My wife took Becky on a horror cattlecall about a year ago," Bobby remembers. When they called her name after a two-hour wait, Becky complained that she was tired and didn't want to go in. My wife said that was okay. The guy yelled Becky's name out again, then said, 'Do you want to go on this interview or not? If not, leave!' She didn't, and they left. The experience cured my wife. She called up Mary Grady and said, 'I don't think she's ready yet.' I said, 'Honey, that's not the way it is with little kids and their agents—the mothers usually call and say, 'Got any work?' Not 'Put a hold on my child!' "

Conscientious parents who leave their children in the business must try to make the best of both worlds. "Good agents learn to work around us, like if there's a soccer game," fifteen-year-old Pat Petersen (*Knots Landing*, 1979–) told me matter-of-factly. But achieving a semblance of normality requires a tolerant agent, a flexible casting director, and a sensitive mother. Alas, such kindly teamwork is rare in Hollywood.

Many parents undoubtedly feel trapped between the responsibilities of childrearing and the desire to enhance their children's careers. They develop attitudinal hypocrisies that even their kids eventually discover. "They wanted me to equally uphold values that they themselves didn't regard equally," former Mouseketeer Darlene Gillespie says of her parents. "Ultimately, show business *was* everything to them. After all, one morning a week my mother pulled me out of grammar school to take me to singing lessons."

Children are saddled with their parents' confused values. "It's not fair for a child to feel he's got to get the part in order for his mother to love him," one agent told me. Fair enough. So how should the stage mother deal with her child in the face of rejection? "I tell them that if someone doesn't want them, they missed the best deal in the world," says Dolores Jacoby. "I tell them that over and over—until it's automatic." But is it effective? "You can't fool people very long," says child psychiatrist Richard Atkins. "The kid may believe it for a while, but how many times can you be told the studio doesn't want you, before you know it's a lie? Parents should support the child's strengths—if he lost the job, how can he make good use of the time it would have taken up? But instead, they tend to focus on the loss."

It is very difficult for an ambitious stage mother to mask disappointment. "When your child hurts, it hurts you doubly," my mother explained to me years after I had stopped acting. I was always aware of how my losses hurt my mother, and how my successes buoyed her spirits. I'll never forget how incredibly excited I was when I was cast in an episode of *Rawhide,* at the age of eleven, because I hadn't worked in seven months. It had been a rough dry period for my mother, and an even rougher one for me. When my agent called to tell me I had the part, I cried from happiness. I was hired for the job without even going on an interview, so I couldn't wait to see the script. But then, what a letdown! Four lines and only a few action scenes. When I discovered that, I again turned on the tears. I wasn't making a comeback, I was forced to realize. My career was indeed on the wane. My mother was so disgusted with my tantrums that, in a rage, she threatened to call my agent to say that I was going to turn down the role. She didn't call, of course; instead, she smacked me hard on the arm. I ran into my bedroom and hid there until dinnertime.

I was furious with her for hitting me, but I also felt guilty for driving her crazy. The business was making me a neurotic mess, and I knew I was inflicting that on her. I was far too young to resent her for putting me in such a vulnerable position originally. When I sheepishly crept out of my room and down the hall to where she was setting the dinner table, I apologized. She put her arms around me and whispered a sentiment that I was far too young to appreciate. "You've got to have a heart of steel in this business." When I once asked her, after all we were forced to endure, why she never pulled me out, she replied, "I didn't think I could have. You would have yelled, screamed, carried on. I didn't want to be the one to take it away from you. You might have blamed me if I had forbidden you to continue going on calls. I wanted to be a good mother and give you freedom of choice."

When the child actor's star begins to recede, he takes his mother back to earth with him. The end can be even more traumatic for her than for her child. She returns to a world that is strange and lonely; to a husband who has shared the most vital years of her life only from afar; to her other children whose lives,

comparatively speaking, lack glamour and a sense of purpose;
to the doldrums of the home life and television soap operas
from which she fled.

The thrill of being on the set is a tough act to follow. I
recall the day I walked onto the set where I was to film the
opening show of the 1963 season of the TV western *Death Valley
Days* (1952–1970). It was one of my very few non-ethnic roles.
I played an all-American farmgirl who gets to meet Brazilian
royalty visiting the West. We assumed that my leading man
would be a moderately successful Spanish character actor. My
mother's jaw dropped when we walked on the set and saw
Gilbert Roland sitting in his make-up chair. Like most child
actors, however, I was far less impressed by many of the stars
with whom I worked. At the age of ten, this was the first time
I had even heard of Gilbert Roland. My idea of a famous name
was a television hero like Richard Chamberlain (*Dr. Kildare*,
1961–1966) or Harry Morgan (Pete of *Pete and Gladys*, 1960–
1962). But my mother sure knew who Gilbert Roland was.
"Being on the set was interesting and fun, something to do
instead of being in the house with the kids, when the big outing
is going to the market at night," she told me with complete
candor. "People can get so excited over footprints at Grauman's
Chinese Theater, so imagine, to actually see these stars! And
to see your daughter on the same set!" Says Cecile Provost,
some twenty years after her son Jon's career ended, "I miss it
so . . . the glamour, the parades. . . . When it ended, I learned
to stay home. It drove me crazy for a while. But Jon's career
brought me a life I couldn't otherwise have had now in the
entertainment field."

Cecile was referring to her activities with an organization
known as the Motion Picture Mothers. Founded in 1939, early
members of the club included mothers of some of the most
memorable child actors and actresses of all time, such as Mickey
Rooney and Judy Garland. Today as then, the members of
Motion Picture Mothers share one overwhelmingly powerful
and loving bond: their children have worked in the entertainment field at one time or another. Motion Picture Mothers al-

lows some ex-stage mothers to continue to flirt with the world from which they have been forcibly wrenched. They raise money for the Motion Picture and Television fund; make guest appearances as star mothers on shows like *The Hollywood Squares* and *The Merv Griffin Show;* and throw Christmas parties at which their children, many of whom are full-grown, perform. But the club is more like Alcoholics Anonymous than Club Med. It is no substitute for the real thing.

There *are* some exceptional mothers who are actually pleased to see their children's careers wind down. They never realized how time-consuming and emotionally draining the involvement would prove to be. Tired of languishing in their children's shadows, they welcome the newfound opportunity to pursue their own careers. Says Tom Rettig, "To sacrifice a great deal of yourself for your children is a great waste of human potential." More to the point, Louise LaRue, mother of Dwayne and Darryl Hickman, once confessed her deepest fear to a friend. "I don't want to be known only for my children."

In my own case, my mother found my fade-out far less painful than she had expected. "At the studios, everything was vicarious," she told me. "I felt proud that this was my offspring, but it wasn't *me*. But through acting I had gotten a taste of something else. I realized there was an outside world and that everything wasn't little babies. So I went into market research. It gave me independence, and a paycheck I earned myself that I had no guilt about spending." She had had her fill of studio glamour, and her fascination for stars was on the wane. Still, she remains thankful. "Without my child's career," she says, "I might have been a housewife all my life."

three

Children on Commission

L inda's career seemed to be going nowhere, but not because she hadn't started early enough. When her father sent her first publicity snapshot around to top children's agents in Los Angeles, she was precisely one day old, still in the hospital. He updated the photo submissions every three months, but no one called. Increasingly restless about her career and worried that the hour was growing late, one morning he took Linda on an agency run.

Their first stop was the Mary Grady Agency; if not the best talent shop in Hollywood, hers was certainly one of the most well-established. MGA has been churning out child actors about as long as Volkswagen has been punching out small cars. Linda's ambitious dad knew that Grady had sold a lot of kids.

They arrived at MGA with high hopes, but the receptionist quickly deflated them. Without an appointment, she said, Grady would not see Linda. Refusing to take no for an answer, her father threatened to camp on the couch all day if they had to.

"There's only one way out of this office," he sneered, pointing to the door connecting the reception area and the interior offices, "and Grady has to come through it." The experienced receptionist had turned back many a pushy parent in her time, but the desperate tone of this man's voice alarmed her. With a curt nod, she excused herself and went inside. She returned to the outer office a few minutes later to fetch Linda for an unscheduled meeting with her boss.

Nearly a half hour had passed with Linda inside, and her father began to fantasize the worst in the style of lurid tabloid headlines. "She's so irresistibly beautiful, who knows what might happen when strangers lay eyes on her?" he thought, paranoia locked in a duel with common sense.

Finally, the receptionist summoned him inside. Linda was on the floor, hugging another client's dog. The agent was looking on approvingly. The receptionist smiled broadly. "She's so gorgeous," the imperious Grady exclaimed. "Why didn't you bring her in here before? You'll definitely hear from us."

The receptionist led the newly discovered star and her proud father out of the agency. After she waved goodbye, his mood abruptly switched from elation to paranoia. One had to be a fool, he thought, to trust the assurance of an agent. You have to keep pushing to make it.

The father-and-daughter duo then proceeded to the Dorothy Day Otis/Jack Rose Agency on Sunset Boulevard. Linda was exceptionally gorgeous and very hireable, they were told. In and out in fifteen minutes.

Then a twenty-minute drive to the Wormser, Heldfond & Joseph Agency, near the Hollywood Bowl. The hour was close to noon; Linda was tiring fast. To refuel, they checked in at another famous Hollywood monument, McDonald's. Linda nibbled on a handful of fries and slurped a few ounces of Coke, but without gusto. The strain of the morning was taking a heavy toll on her.

Entering the office building where Wormser, Heldfond & Joseph was headquartered, Linda began to nod off. Her father was concerned; he was afraid she would put the agents to sleep too. He needed one more burst of sunshine from her.

Carrying her briskly past the WHJ doors, he searched for a water fountain. There was one down the hall. Positioning Linda's face over the faucet, he turned it on and began scooping machine-cooled water toward her face until it streamed down in little rivers. Linda stirred, her beautiful dark eyes opening wide, a lovely fawn caught in a sudden shower. Linda was now alert and ready for her next audition. She had better be. At eight *months* of age, this was no time to act like a baby.

Hollywood's baby business is highly competitive. There are not a great many TV and movie roles for kids under four. The lucky few who get work are often hired by word of mouth. Usually at the last minute, the baby of a parent in the cast or crew is summoned in for a quick smile-on, or cry-on. In Hollywood, few babies make it into agents' files, and fewer still are ever actually signed as clients. Those who do are recruited in a relatively casual manner.

One common scouting site is the pediatrician's office. An agent might ask a nurse at the doctor's office to contact her when a particularly adorable baby patient appears. The doctor himself might be supplied with the agent's business cards to hand out to an attractive patient's parents.

The baby may become a client even before the agency lays eyes on him. As one agent explains it, "I've had pregnant mothers who are clients say to me, 'Will you represent my child?' " At this point, of course, the future client is in no position to object. At the age of fifteen *days*, a baby is eligible for an official State of California work permit.

In New York, the advertising center of the nation and the home of hundreds of national firms that advertise heavily on TV, babies still in diapers are in great demand. The promotion of products like talcum powder, baby food and diapers provides abundant job opportunities. But even around Madison Avenue, a photogenic baby can go crying for an agent. "A lot of agents and managers don't like to represent them," explains Arline McGovern of New York's Goodwin & McGovern Management, one of the few outfits specializing in newborns. "They're a pain. They get sick. They're unreliable." And between the ages of fifteen to eighteen months they are forced, in effect, to retire. "At that age, they begin to rebel," explains one New York children's manager. "They start to have minds of their own."

They're also changeable and moody. One month they love to be cuddled by everyone, say agents, the next they don't want to be touched by anybody. Babies with winning smiles suddenly become criers. To cover all prospective bets, agents maintain large stockpiles of freshly minted tots to replace the ones who go sour. A New York baby agent and manager may have a kiddie clientele numbering in the hundreds. Fewer than sixty or seventy is too shallow a talent pool.

An agency's baby catalogue must contain all sizes and shapes. "They order a baby by inches or pounds," explains Suzanne Schachter of the New York children's management firm Suzelle. "They call up and say, 'I want a six-month-old baby who doesn't weigh more than twenty pounds, can't crawl, has no teeth, and has X amount of hair on its head.' " It is considered prudent planning to keep on file at least ten in all of the less mobile age brackets (including three to five months, five to eight months, and nine to eleven months), and ten walkers (eleven to thirteen months). It is also common to develop an even distribution of sexes, though girls are preferable for the nude shot and for the call requesting a baby size of small.

This is one job market in which there is no sex discrimination of any kind. The best-looking baby body will be bundled off to the job. One New York casting director told me that, in the course of searching for a feminine, gentle-looking baby to star in an Ivory soap commercial, the softest-looking baby to audition happened to be a boy. So he took the boy, put him in a dress, and placed him before the camera. "That's normal," he insists.

Successful New York baby managers scout for talent by placing ads in local newspapers and trade papers like *Show*

Business, the East Coast version of the *Hollywood Reporter* and *Daily Variety.* They also stay on the lookout for fresh faces wherever they go. "I may spot a baby in Macy's," hypothesizes McGovern. "I once spotted one licking an ice cream cone. I ran over to the mother, gave her my name, and said, 'Have you ever thought of your baby doing commercials?' Then I gave her my card and said, 'Give us a call.' "

She did. "They almost always call," she says. "Then they ask, 'How much money do I have to lay out?' I say, 'You just do the commercial and we get our fifteen per cent commission.' The next question is, 'What type of work do you *really* do?' They're afraid of pornography."

But a mother's hopes almost always overshadow her fears. When baby managers hold open calls, normally 200–300 mothers and infants can be counted on to show up. If there were no screener stationed at the door to reject the ones who obviously have no chance, the call would soon become a mob scene. The screener is usually instructed to let through the WASPy, all-American-looking darlings of the advertising world referred to as "blonde baldies." Also valued are the red-heads, deemed rare specimens (baby hair generally does not turn rusty until around one and a half years of age). Sandy-haired babies stand a fairly good chance of getting inside, but the very dark-haired ones do not. As one children's manager explained, "Those representing Luvs and Huggies diapers may go for the sandy-haired babies, but not super-dark ones."

Inside the screening, the merchandise is inspected with microscopic attention to detail. The discovery of the tiniest mole on the head will prompt the rejection of the cutest blonde baldie. A birthmark on the face will hurt his chances, and a birthmark on the baby's behind will rule him out for diaper commercials. But big bottoms are a plus. Says New York agent Judy Klein, "For diaper commercials, you need some who aren't scrawny, with nice, round little thighs."

At these sessions, the managers take no one's word for anything. No matter that the mother swears on a stack of holy books that her baby's behind is smooth as a peach or round as a melon; she *must* remove the diaper to prove the point. Mothers do have a reputation for shading the truth. Says McGovern, "I have asked a mother if the baby can walk and she says, 'Sure!' Then I send it on an interview and the casting director is furious because it can't. Or she says her baby utterly adores Jello, then he spits it out in the high chair on the set."

Baby clients require special handling. Naptimes must be flexibly designed; mothers need to schedule them just before the interviews. Agents know that the baby who is deprived of sleep before the call will display a fatal crankiness. The most personal habits are of concern. "I find that I prefer to represent nursing babies," says McGovern, "because they tend to have better personalities and get along well with people."

Personality and intelligence can be important. Agents know from experience that a baby who is quick on the uptake in the office is likely to do well on the set when the commercial is shot. "You want that reaction," says McGovern. "Sometimes you take the baby up to the mirror to see if it wants to touch what it sees, or just stares aimlessly into the blue. Sometimes you tickle the baby. Or you pull the bottle away from him to see if he gets upset. After all, on some commercials they want them to cry." Requirements vary. New York agent Judy Klein demands that her clients be cheerful. "If it isn't friendly," she says, "and he cries for his mother, it's bye-bye, baby."

New York manager Marianne Leone of Terrific Talent Associates, Inc., which maintains a small but prosperous baby department, has her own guidelines. "Babies who are third or fourth siblings tend to be more outgoing," she explains. "Mothers of firstborns are more apt to cuddle their babies, so they are more withdrawn. I make sure to ask the mothers how many are in the family and which one this particular child is in the line." If these agents and managers seem fussy, they can afford to be. "I never suffer from a shortage of clients," says New York manager Suzanne Schachter, "because babies are always being born."

"You've seen a bunch of losers today," the casting director told me apologetically at the end of an audition for a Pampers diaper commercial. He was looking for a baby, male or female, under age one, weighing between sixteen and twenty-three pounds. It was a choice part, and for several days New York agents and managers had been sending mothers and babies to the audition at the Manhattan studio. For any one commercial role, hundreds of babies are interviewed, and four are usually booked. The final decision about which one will be the commercial star is rarely made until all four babies are lined up on the set the morning of the shoot. The other three, called "back-up" babies, are paid $300 apiece to stand by in case the principal performer starts to act his age.

But to find four competent performers, casting directors usually have to weed through as many as 100 babies. To increase the likelihood of having at least one client land the job, they send out as many babies as they can. As one New York children's manager put it, "The infant mortality rate in this business is unbelievably high." New York commercial casting directors will almost invariably audition a baby twice, on separate days, to obtain an accurate sampling of its moods. The mother is never permitted to watch.

The studio where the diaper audition was held that day looked like a pediatrician's office. Its bright pink waiting room walls were decorated with animal cartoons; a soft blanket covered a plastic table to facilitate the changing of diapers; and the audition room was packed with an array of hobby horses, dolls, toy telephones, even a maroon velvet high chair. Lights and cameras surrounded a white plastic table with padding underneath (plastic makes it easier to clean up after non-potty-trained contestants) where the babies who made it to the callback were to be photographed.

This diaper commercial was demanding. The script called for a baby to lie on its back and smile while Mother changes his diaper. But infinitely malleable babies are made, not born. Carefully and tenderly, the casting director cooed to the babies and played with their hands and feet to win them over. Most responded to his overtures with ear-piercing wails. "I've done nothing to bring the crying on," the casting director said in despair when one baby, clutching onto a yellow plastic duck for dear life, let out a scream. "She's not going to be comfortable on a TV set." Next!

Mothers can be as childish as their babies. When one young unwed Chicano mother heard the sound of her baby erupting into tears inside the audition room, she, too, started to bawl. "You made me come all the way here for nothing!" she screamed at her eight-month-old son when the casting director brought him back. Another mother had a most novel excuse for her baby daughter's outburst. "She's suspicious of men," she explained to the casting director. "*She's* the one who's suspicious of men," the casting director said with disgust after the pair left. "The baby's just a clinger. But you never tell a mother something like that or you get killed!"

All instantaneous criers' names were scratched off the list and immediately returned to their mothers' arms. "No back" babies, who refused to lie happily on their backs for the director, were also weeded out. "These are normal, average kids," the casting director admitted. "We have to find the special ones." Agents often complicate an audition by sending babies who are wrong for the role. One baby on this diaper call was too old (she was almost one). One was too fat (over twenty-three pounds). Another was what is known as an HH—"hand-hold only"—baby. "Sometimes you wonder if you should give up," the HH's mother sighed. "Do you think she's good?" Feigning mild enthusiasm, the casting director said, "Yes, she's good." The baby's father was deeply offended. "Not good, *very* good," he snapped.

Then, as if by a miracle, in walked the dream of every mother, director, and agent: a pure-bred blond baldie in a fancy white taffeta dress. The casting director jerked into action, administering rigorous tests, swinging the blonde baldie back and forth in his arms, even tilting her upside down, to test her reaction. But she continued to giggle and smile as if undergoing the most pleasurable experience. "She's wholesome!" he exclaimed. "She's remote control!"

A blonde baldie had done it again. All the others were told to go home. "I get let down every time," said the last mother whose baby cried, her own eyes brimming with tears.

The heavy-set German woman wearing a floppy Hedda Hopper–style hat pointed to the center of the herd of babies at the kiddie cattlecall and, as if with pride of parentage, told the mother beside her, "Those six are mine."

"But that's impossible!" the mother exclaimed. "They're all the same age!"

It wasn't impossible. The grand dame at the casting call, former Universal Studios screenwriter Lola Moore, was not their mother, but their agent. The kind who usually mothers all her clients. She was also a noted trailblazer. In the 1920s, only Moore and a man named Harry Weber, an old-time vaudeville and film agent who managed Mickey Rooney for a time, specialized in representing children.

In those days, mothers did not need agents. They saw no real reason to forfeit that ten per cent commission. The movie world was small, and children could find work without them. Jane Withers, for example, did not sign with an agent until the age of seven, after she had inked her Twentieth Century Fox contract and had gotten to be so big a star that she had to have one. Even then, Withers says, her mother remained the chief orchestrator of her career.

That was an era when mothers had even more leverage on their children's careers than they do today. It was Margaret O'Brien's mother, not her agent, who walked into Louis B. Mayer's office while her daughter was working on *Meet Me in St. Louis* (1944) and threatened to pull her off the picture unless Mayer agreed to raise Margaret's salary. And it was her mother, she says, who was largely responsible for her landing the *Journey for Margaret* role (1942) that made her a star. "It was a huge casting call, but I got it because I had talent and I had a smarter mother who knew who to talk to," she says.

In a motherly style, Lola Moore pioneered the children's agenting business. At Christmas, she would invite them over to her old, cluttered house atop the Hollywood Hills to help her make jam. They would package the delicious homemade spread in her array of antique vases and jars. Then one by one, she would send her top kiddie clients to the major studios around town to present the jars as gifts to the casting directors. It was of course the kids, not the jam, that Moore was hoping they would develop a taste for.

Although I never attended any of Lola's jam sessions, she somehow developed a taste for me, and became my first agent. Of course, at one time or another, she seemed to have been nearly everyone's first agent; her client list was usually several hundred kids long. "She played her cards kind of wild," my mother remembers. "She figured out of all those numbers, she'd get something."

But kids never had to be dragged to Lola Moore's house. Not to that toy-cluttered menagerie of cats, dogs, live chicks on Easter, and finger-licking good jam at Christmas! Mothers were charmed by her act, too. Lola held round-the-clock coffee klatches where they could gab for hours until someone would telephone her with a casting call. Then she would shoo them home so they could race their kids to the studios. "She was very devoted to her clientele, if you really wanted your child to work and you went along with her ways," says Cecile Provost, whose son Jon was represented by Lola throughout his success-studded career.

But in time, Lola Moore's inimitably warm, motherly style of agenting went the way of the Hollywood studio system. She hung on for as long as she could, then the agency closed its doors. Today the representation of children has become a less personal, mass business. There are dozens of very active children's agents in Hollywood, promoting many thousands of children. Some represent kids exclusively, others run "young people's" departments within well-established adult actors' agencies. Beyond numbers, however, there is another reason for the proliferation of children's agents, even though the representation of adults is considered more prestigious. "We stage mothers don't die out," explains Evelyn Schultz of Wormser,

Heldfond & Joseph. "We become agents." Once infected by the business, there is rarely a cure. The addiction tends to be lifelong. Agenting is a marvelous remedy for the withdrawal pain a mother feels over the loss of her child's career. "I miss the set," admits ex-stage mother Doris Ross of the Associated Talent Agency. "I guess being an agent is the closest I could get to being there."

A mother's decision to become an agent is born of desperation as much as ambition. What else is the disenfranchised stage mother to do? She doesn't want to watch the daytime soaps, she wants to be in them, or at least help cast them! She is eager to work. But what does she have to offer the general job market? Youth? Mastery of sophisticated business skills? There is only one thing she can do better than anyone else— sell kids. "Sitting on the sets taught me about the kinds of kids they use," says Hollywood agent Toni Kelman. She is unruffled when her son reproaches her for staying on in the business he so eagerly abandoned. "They're going to use kids no matter what," she tells him. "So why shouldn't I do something I enjoy? The business has been good for me, and I've been good for the business."

It is easier to get ahead in agenting if your child was once a star. "When I got remarried, I had a different name than my daughter," says Nina Tobin. Her daughter Michele was a well-known child star from TV series like *The Fitzpatricks* (1977–1978) and *Grandpa Goes to Washington* (1978–1979). "I couldn't get my foot in the door as a manager. I changed my name back to Tobin, and everything clicked after that. I got in as my daughter's mother."

Given the relatively brief duration of the average child actor's career, the daughter's mother has to act fast. More independently career-oriented than the mother of yesteryear, she may make the transition before the child's career begins to decline. Motivated by the money her kids are bringing in, she puts together a Rolodex of young clients as a new profit source. She may even represent her own offspring. "I am like a client to my mother," says twelve-year-old Shane Butterworth (*Bad*

News Bears, 1979–1980; *Exorcist II: The Heretic*, 1977), son of Los Angeles manager Tami Lynn. In effect echoing the reassurance his mother gives the parents of other clients, Shane says, "She likes to see me work, but she likes to see her other clients work too."

New York agent Judy Klein insists that an agent/mother must maintain a businesslike attitude toward her kids. "If I have babies who are better-looking or who have better dispositions than mine, those babies go on interviews," she says. "But my husband protests. He's a stage father. He thinks no child is as good as his. But I want my professional reputation upheld!" Managing the child's career can put unexpected strains on family life. It can be made to work, but a tremendous level of maturity is required.

"There was a lot of pressure on me because my mother was an agent," says former New York child performer Bonnie Shulman. "I had to do things right for the first time because of the family reputation." In the late forties and early fifties, Bonnie enjoyed a prosperous career as a model and as a radio and TV commercial performer. At the age of thirteen, she packed it in. Until recently, she represented children at the respected New York agency Marje Fields, Inc. "I have an impetus to change things. I want to work to protect the children," says Shulman. She actively promotes entertainment children's rights by participating in negotiating Screen Actors Guild contracts that may set new precedents for child actors in the state of New York, and advocates the revision of the state's work permit regulations for performing minors. These are notoriously lax and all too infrequently enforced rules (see Chapter Five). "Having been a child performer," says Shulman, "has given me empathy."

Ex-child stars, like former stage mothers, bring a special background to the trade. "I have an eye for the kinds of kids they want," says Iris Burton, now a topnotch children's agent. Iris was only seven when her mother, a Ziegfeld Follies beauty, entered her in the New York *Daily News* Beautiful Child Contest. She won, and went on to modeling, then musical comedy.

Many years later, when she joined the ranks of divorcées looking for work, she knew precisely how to capitalize on her early achievements. "You have to give them today's kid," says Burton, "one who can get out, put in eight hours of work, know his lines, not be restless on the set, and behave like a professional."

Some people become children's agents simply because they love kids, no strings attached. Says one, "Children make ideal clients because they're not so desperate for money." Says another, "They have no guile."

"Is Jeannine now forty-seven inches exactly?" a woman's voice yelled out over the ringing of a multitude of telephones.

"Close enough!" another voice screamed back.

"And how are her teeth? In or out?"

The setting for this exchange of technical information regarding a client was a top children's agency located on Sunset Boulevard in Hollywood. In process was the day's updating of the office file, to keep pace with clients who literally grow new statistics day by day. Children's agents have many changes to monitor: height (measured in fractions of the inch, not gross feet); weight (reregistered with every few new pounds); skin (acned or clear?); eyes (has the child gotten glasses, or does he still have good vision?); reading skills (has he acquired them, or is he still too young?). And those ever-mercurial dispositions! Is the child going through the phase of "loving the business"? Or is he now telling Mommy he "wants out"? Is he more likely to show up promptly for the baseball tryout than for the cereal commercial?

An agency will have other pressing concerns: keeping up contact with casting directors; sending the right kids on the right interviews; applying follow-up pressure on the casting directors when the kids leave; negotiating for money. It is a complex operation. In New York, the children's agent often will share the workload with a number of managers, who work as kind of sub-agents. The casting director will inform the agent of the call. The agent in turn gives the call to a number of managers with whom she shares business. Then the manager tells the parents. In Hollywood, managers are just beginning to emerge as a major force in the business. They offer more personal services than agents. They also pressure agents to send the clients they share in common on interviews. In Hollywood, although casting directors deal primarily with agents (managers are not franchised by the Screen Actors Guild and only agents have the authority to send children on calls), a manager's fee is fifteen per cent compared to an agent's ten per cent. By comparison to a manager, who will have only a handful of clients, some agents handle up to 100 kids, making it impossible for any one child to receive much personal attention.

Of course, that level of attention may matter more to the mother than to the child. "Be at a Burger King commercial at such and such studio at four-fifteen!" your typical Hollywood agent barks, just before slamming down the phone. The mother then flies into a panic. How should my child be dressed? What age should he say he is at the interview? What pictures should he bring? The lack of tranquility in the mother can infect the child with the jitters. "I told one of my mothers to take Valium," recalls manager Nina Tobin. "I said, 'You're nervous and it's wearing off on the kids. So they're not picking up work!' "

Managers may wind up supervising the mother as much as the child. "Managers can direct things better than I can," explains the mother of a four-year-old girl already on her fourth agent. "I brought everything on my daughter's clothes rack to her manager's home and laid it out on her two sofas. The manager calls these audition clothes 'uniforms.' She has categories for the entire wardrobe. There's the baby-doll category and the very commercial, schoolgirl category. When she sends my daughter out on a commercial she'll say, for example, 'It's not just cute and coy,' or 'They want a tomboy; put on her overalls, a striped shirt, white sneakers.' I don't want to have to stop and think whether we've got the clothes. I want to be ready to go to the interview." When necessary, this same manager may supply her clients with outfits she keeps stored in her own home. "I spot check the kids once a month," she says, "even my really hot clients, so that I know their wardrobes are up-to-date."

The manager's forte is personalized career guidance, even to the point of serving as a consultant in areas of hair-splitting concern. Nina Tobin meets her little girls and their mothers at various beauty parlors around town to help choose the ideal haircuts for the children. "You have to give people *something* for their fifteen per cent," she told me. Managers are supposed to remain available to the mothers almost around-the-clock. "You can't reach an agent before ten," points out Tobin. "I get phone calls twenty-four hours a day." They may drive their clients to interviews when their mothers are busy. They keep track of the kids' incomes and at the end of the year present their mothers with balance sheets. They explain to the mothers how to evaluate contracts. They check TV and movie sets to make sure the mothers and children share a private dressing room, or, at the very least, have a trailer all to themselves. They unfailingly call their clients after their television and movie appearances to rave about their performances, especially the bad ones.

Where there is severe mother-daughter tension, managers can play a mediative role. The child may be more willing to listen to the manager than the mother. The manager may even advise her teenaged female clients on how to apply make-up properly. The most common advice is: no make-up. "Only Brooke Shields is the exception," says one of today's top Hollywood child managers.

The manager may offer private acting lessons to her clients. Los Angeles manager Jean Page provides last-minute schooling before an interview. If five kids whom she represents are going out on the same interview, she drives the group herself and coaches them on the way. "If I say 'Jump,' they jump," she boasts. "And they jump because I'm good to them. I always have goodies in the car. We sing songs, tell jokes. There's a method in that. Very often a child will go on a call and the casting director will say, 'Sing a song,' and the child says, 'I don't know a song.' . . . I try to smooth out their rough edges by thorough preparation."

Negotiating salaries for child actors can be very tricky. Managers like to think of themselves as tougher than agents, who are too busy, they say, to quibble over the bottom dollar. "Agents never ask for enough money," complains Los Angeles manager Tami Lynn. "They'd rather have ten per cent of something than nothing."

That something may be less than it should be. Although the money in the children's acting business is always good and sometimes very good, it rarely equals adult pay scales. Producers have a bias, whether conscious or not, against paying top dollar. "They figure Robert Redford is not replaceable," says Jean Page, "but a lot of kids are." Says former children's agent Dorothy Day Otis, "When I negotiated I would always have to say, 'Look, he may be a little short in height, but he's still an actor.' " The desperate mother can work against a child's best financial interests, too. Explains a representative in the children's department of the Herb Tannen Agency in Los Angeles, "When a mother is scared because her kid only worked twelve times this year, she warns me, 'Don't lose the job!' I love it when a mother says, 'Tell them to get stuffed!' "

The kids get shorted in other ways. Consider the matter of billing, which is a measure of achievement for any actor. Major billing increases the chances of getting the next part. To display an actor's name prominently is akin to putting money in the bank. But kids rarely get credit commensurate with their contributions. "You can always get feature billing, but if you are going for costar billing, the kid has to have ten credits for any one adult's credit," says agent Doris Ross.

To a child, top billing is better than a straight-A report card. He may be utterly unimpressed by the overall magnificence of his career, and he may never lay eyes (or hands) on his own bank account. But, oh, how he loves to see his name appear on the screen, in big, bold lettering! "If someone shuts the TV off before the credits at the end," one twelve-year-old boy told me, "I put it back on."

At the center of all this haggling among agents, managers and producers about billing and money is an innocent child who very often does not understand the rules of the game. Former child actor Gary Marsh remembers that on the seventh and last callback for the part of Tom in the movie *Camelot* (1967), the men interviewing him offered their congratulations for getting the part. "I was so ecstatic I came home and did flips," he remembers. "Then my agent said I didn't have a part. It crushed me. I cried. What I didn't realize was that they were still in the process of negotiating. They hadn't settled on a price, so technically I didn't have the part." He eventually did get the role, but psychologically it may have cost him more than he was paid. The incident led him to believe that one could never trust an agent or producer at his word, that you could have a part one minute but lose it the next, and that his worth as a person was being measured by some very subjective, and changeable, standards. "That experience made me a lot harder," he says today.

In the acting business, children become old quickly. "In at six, out at ten" is the motto of the children's department of Wormser, Heldfond & Joseph. Every agent needs a good distribution of kids within the age range that sells best, the six to ten year olds, and children under age six change so rapidly that the agency maintains separate age categories for every chronological year.

Only a few budding Mickey Rooneys and Shirley Temples in age categories one, two, three, four and five are ordinarily required to cover an agency's needs. From age six on up, the children are sorted out in two-year classifications, in accordance with their slowing changes in physical size and emotional characteristics. Whom an agent accepts as a client often depends upon whom she already has in stock. The agent who is low on eight year olds, for example, may accept a mediocre nine year old over a perfect ten. The age the agency markets the child at may have little to do with his date of birth, however. A more crucial consideration is his height and overall appearance. A ten year old who has already grown sixty inches tall will be sent on auditions calling for kids aged eleven or even twelve. The six year old who is only forty inches high can be sold as a four year old.

I'll never forget my mother's hurt and rage when she opened up my second agent's new directory of clients and saw that underneath my photo I was listed as nine years old, my real age. To make matters worse, several of my rivals, who were also age nine but looked to her about eighteen, had been listed as eight. This was a devastating development, for the longer you can look younger, the longer you can work. My mother confronted the agent directly about it, but the agent told her to bug off and snapped, "Andrea's face is older." That is perhaps the worst news an agent can bring to a child actor's mother.

The other major selling point for the agent is a kid's "type." Always quick to grab up the mature but still wholesome all-American ex-blonde baldies or red-headed commercial children, today's casting directors are, however, warming up slightly to more exotic looks. "They call the new type the Spice of Life kid," explains New York agent Marcia Goldenberg of MMG Enterprises, Ltd./Marcia's Kids. "That means Waspy, but not white bread." Character kids are gaining in employability. "They can be way out, with glasses, hair standing on end, even buck teeth," says Evelyn Schultz. "But if he's really fat, he's not going to work as much because they won't buy him for food, drinks, candy or take-out food commercials." Only on a rare occasion will a fat kid provide the agent with a sale. Remember Mason Reese, the chubby little boy with the owlish face who made it big in the early seventies doing a series of commercials advertising Underwood meat spreads? Says Al Criado of Hollywood's Dale Garrick, International agency, "A fat kid is a specialty, like having a mime artist."

Agents are always scrambling to turn out human clichés to appeal to casting directors. One of the most popular is the so-called fresh, innocent type, the inexperienced kid untainted by overexposure, either to success or failure. That kind of order may elicit a snicker from the agent. "I get upset when they say,

'Send us a real kid, not a Hollywood kid,' " says Joy Stevenson of Harry Gold and Associates in Los Angeles. "What am I supposed to—pick up a kid off the street? If I do, chances are he can't read a script!"

In these times, every contemporary agent tries to get hold of a few "street-wise" types. Some recruit directly from black ghettos. Black kids with the wholesome middle-class look do not meet the needs of today's clichés. "I have to instruct my [middle-class] black kids how to be streetwise," complains one Hollywood agent. "I tell them to dress like thugs, wear Levis, cut-off jackets, and handkerchiefs in their back pockets. Some of their mothers have to go out and buy those things." Agents prefer the "real McCoy," which is easiest to spot in places like Watts in Los Angeles, or Brooklyn and Queens in New York City.

Says agent Jim Bridges, father of Todd Bridges, one of Gary Coleman's costars on the TV series *Diff'rent Strokes* (1978–), "As the father of a star, I know my son feels he has to be twice as good as a white kid to win out." In 1974, Bridges, a former actor himself, his three acting children and his actress/wife became the first black family to do a commercial together (for Jello gelatin). In 1977, Bridges quit acting to become an agent. After a short stint with the Mary Grady Agency, he left to open up his own agency. His problems at MGA were the obvious ones. "Calls would come into the office from a casting director for which no race specification was made, but no one would have the guts to ask, 'Are you using ethnic groups?' White agents say it's bad policy to do that up front. But a lot of times casting directors don't even know you represent blacks until you call it to their attention! I've seen them go black although at first they didn't think of going anything but white. But when advertising representatives say they want Midwestern types only, that means one thing—white."

Bridges is one of the few black agents in Hollywood representing a large, but not exclusively, black child and adult clientele. Still, it is very hard, he says, to keep his business afloat. The ethnic agent has even less leverage in negotiating money for a kid who isn't white. They tend to be offered flat up-front fees, at which point the discussion is left on a take-it-or-leave-it basis. Negotiating an audition can be trickier than settling on a fee. Sometimes, Bridges says, in order to provide the illusion of granting equal opportunity, they'll consent to interview black kids, all the while knowing they'll "go white."

Ghetto kids are paradoxically easy to sell and difficult to represent. If their parents don't own cars, they don't make it to interviews on time, if at all. It is a long ride from Watts to Hollywood, in more ways than one. And it is not easy to sell a client who can't afford the conventional apparatus to help sell himself. Parents of "real" ghetto kids may not be able to spare several hundred dollars for a good set of photographs or an acting course. These economic hardships place extra pressure on the agent. Doris Ross remembers losing as a client a poverty-stricken twelve-year-old black boy whose career was beginning to pick up. But when he couldn't even afford to buy a set of gym clothes for his physical education course at junior high school, he got a failing grade and was denied a state work permit. The loss of the permit mugged his sense of self-esteem. "The last thing we heard," says Ross, "he was put in a juvenile home."

Non-Caucasian children never have an easy ride. Hollywood agent Freda Granite, a South American woman who represents chiefly Hispanics and Indians, faces similar problems with her clients involving inadequate funds, transportation and job opportunities. Hispanic kids are stereotyped even more than blacks, if that's possible. In Hollywood's eyes, everyone south of the border needs to look like a relative of Carmen Miranda. "I can't market my light-haired ones," Granite complains.

Minority kids tend not to sell themselves aggressively enough. "Hollywood needs that outgoing, independent kid who can handle himself," explains Granite, "but Hispanics, Indians and Orientals are basically shy and introverted." Similarly, the parents of minority kids regard the business with suspicion or ignorance. "*We* have to pursue *them*," says agent

Joy Stevenson. "And unlike most of our other parents, they aren't pushy enough. We call for interviews and the mother says, 'Which business are you talking about?' "

Asian parents maintain a deeply embedded value system that is much different from Hollywood's. Guy Lee of the Bessie Loo Agency, who specializes in clients from the Asian Pacific, says that Asian parents are largely apathetic. But while most of his colleagues find that attitude incomprehensible, Lee is understanding. "Parents realize the life span of a child actor is short, and that there's too much risk involved. The parents would rather the children prepare for school and a secure life than chase after a Hollywood dream."

The agent or manager looking to secure a place for herself in the market may resort to almost anything to attract attention. When the Long Island–based Sunshine Talent Reps, Inc., opened its doors a few years ago, manager Maria Brescio was desperate for a gimmick. One finally came to her. With a flurry of ads in the local papers, Sunshine Talent Reps put out the flag as an agency representing . . . twins! It worked; doors opened wide, and today Brescio manages some fifty pairs of identical twins. Since infants are so unpredictable and no one can be relied upon to give a command performance, twins come in handy because if one becomes tired and cranky in the course of filming, the other can be substituted. They have another capability. Babies between the ages of fifteen days and six months are permitted to work only twenty minutes a day, and they may not be exposed to lights on the set for more than thirty *seconds* at a time (with the studio teacher/child labor representative actually timing the shooting with a stopwatch). Identical twins double a director's working time, if not his pleasure. On TV episodes that are filmed before live audiences, both twins may participate in rehearsals. Just before the curtain goes up, the director will select the one in the better mood. On the hit ABC sit-com *Too Close for Comfort* (1980–), the baby son born to Muriel and Henry Rush is played by identical twins.

By this logic, identical triplets are, as Brescio put it, "a three-time useful product." But they are so hard to find! Those who simply resemble one another, but are not identical (i.e., interchangeable) have no special value in the marketplace. Usually. Who would have guessed that in the opening scene of the movie *Superman* (1978), in which the baby's parents (played by Marlon Brando and Susannah York) send their child skyrocketing from Krypton to planet Earth, the infant Superman was played by a pair of babies in alternating shots who were neither twins, nor the same sex, though they looked as if they were.

The agent just getting started knows that mothers of successful kids are locked up by the well-known agents. So they concentrate their efforts on the parents of newcomers, even total unknowns. For that much sought-after "real" kid who can be found at the public schools, Hollywood agent Toni Kelman recruited clients early in her career by prowling around her son's old school. After first securing the permission of the elementary school principal, she'd stake out the schoolyard, spot a saleable-looking kid, point him out to the principal, take down his name and home phone number, and telephone the parents with the news that she was about to make their son, or daughter, a star.

Kelman's prowl was not confined to her son's predominantly white, upper-middle-class school. While this was an enclave of all-American-looking types, she was also hoping to enroll at least one Chicano child. To round out her client list, she hung out at a school located in a ghetto area of Los Angeles like some freelancing marijuana dealer.

The highs she was offering were perfectly legal, of course, if every bit as addicting. All over Los Angeles, there may be children's agents lurking in the bushes. "They think I'm there to supervise reading," says manager Jean Page, who stalks the corridors and classrooms of Catholic schools not far from her home in suburban Los Angeles. "I go up and down the aisles and help them with their spelling. I look at their names on their papers." Page's recruiting efforts get the blessing of the schools' good sisters, who take delight in helping to select potential stars. As Page will explain it to them, "Sister Mary, I want two children between the ages of five and ten, bright, who follow directions and listen carefully. Plus, I want them to be shorter than average and look like your all-American kid." In the classroom, Page and a nun, communicating silently via eye contact, will settle on a few good possibilities and then plot an informal audition. The nun will make a point of calling on the prospects during the oral lesson to give Page a feel for their personalities. At the end of class, Page will hand the young prospects her business cards and wait for their parents to call. The response rate? Almost one hundred per cent telephone the next day, or not long thereafter.

The well-established agent or manager doesn't have to slink around school buildings because he's deluged by ambitious parents begging for established representation for their children. The first thing these agents require is a picture. Even then, the odds of being called in for a personal interview are slim. From the 100 pictures the average Hollywood agent receives in the mail each week, she usually consents to see one child. There are simply too many children in the talent pool these days. The supply exceeds the demand, even as the demand continues to grow. In my era, before the child acting game had become a Hollywood mass industry, it was easy to get an agent. If you were cute, reasonably articulate, not too shy and not too tall, someone was sure to gamble on you. And if you were genuinely talented and had a list of credits to your name, the agents welcomed you.

Today, the talented child needs to sell himself to the agent. Don Schwartz, an agent who uses unorthodox methods in selecting kids, declares that the most important part of his preselection process is the test determining the child's level of inhibition. Schwartz believes the inherently inhibited child is inherently unemployable. "I tell the kids to put one foot in one hand and jump around the room laughing," he says. "Believe it or not, many of them can't do that." Other agents may require the child to undergo an in-depth interview to test facets of his personality and talent. "After all, you may invest time and energy in a child, but you don't make a dime until he's sold," says Hollywood agent Althea Shaw of the Glenn Shaw Agency.

The agent must first be convinced that the child's look is right. Now that the old-style Shirley Temple cutie-pie look is out and the natural-kid look is in, agents prefer the child to show up wearing casual school clothes. Only if the look is saleable will a personality test be administered. It is then that the parent, if not the child, will notice that the agent can be amazingly fussy. "I like a very natural child almost on the verge of being precocious," says Toni Kelman. "There's a fine line between being natural—the kind of kid who sits down and says, 'Hi, how are you?'—and the smart ass one. I like the child who is natural, inquisitive, aware, and outgoing." Natural . . . and on the verge of precociousness?

The agent will talk at considerable length with the child to feel him out. "You try and hit on a subject that makes him sparkle," Kelman says, preferring to develop topics such as the child's hobbies, sports, summer vacations—subjects that distract him from the tension of the interview situation. But the reasonably bright child knows he is on center stage. "He really has to come in and sell me," says Evelyn Schultz. "If he waits to answer and looks to his mother, or answers in monosyllables and won't speak up, there's nothing there, especially for commercials. If a child can't sell me, he's certainly not going to be able to sell the casting person or product."

A lot of kids flunk this part of the test. "You do get youngsters who are a little cautious," says Kelman, who nevertheless tries to give the benefit of the doubt to potential latebloomers. "After all, some of the kids don't even know why they are there. When we ask them if they know, some say, 'To be on TV.' They rarely say movies, because TV is what children watch most. Then, five minutes later, we ask them if they think they'd like to be on TV. Some say no!"

There are occasions when an agent does not want to take no for an answer, of course. The child who looks like a moneymaker must be signed up. "He could say no out of shyness, or because somebody's teased him," Kelman reasons. "He may pull back because he doesn't want to be different." These are not sufficient reasons to flatly rule him out. "It depends on how he says no and what he says about it," she insists. Says agent Al Criado, remembering a child who forcefully insisted he didn't want an acting career, "He was such a charming little boy. Eventually, I got him to think in terms of getting money to buy toys. Then he said, 'Sure, I'd love to do it!' "

Not all children can be bought, however. "When the kids say they don't want to act, I think their mothers beat them," says Evelyn Schultz, only half kiddingly. "I'm sure they at least get a talking-to when they leave. They scold them, berate them, push and shove them, make them feel they're unwanted. There are other ways of beating a child, besides physically. If I tell a mother I really don't think her child wants to do it, she says, 'He's not feeling good today, he really wants to do it, he wakes up in the middle of the night saying, 'Mommy, can I do commercials?' " Just as directors will administer a "parent test" at an audition, agents are similarly wary. "A lot of times I've thought, 'That's a terrific kid!' " says Althea Shaw. "But when I interview the parent, I get turned right off. I can just sense the mother is bringing the child in to satisfy her own needs."

Even if the child is ambitious, talkative, articulate, and has a halfway decent mother, he must demonstrate an ability to handle a script. Most agents keep supplies of old TV series and commercial scripts for the child aged six or over to give an office reading. The three, four or five year old who can't read has to show that he can memorize, or at least mimic, some lines.

When the agent consults the parent, the final stage of the exam has come. If the agent is interested in the child, topics under discussion range from the practical (how to join the Screen Actors Guild) to the personal (why you should not push your child too hard). The child is usually excluded from the final discussions. "Either way, I don't think it's good for him to hear what we have to say," says Kelman. A good thing, because the agent's advice can be quite severe. One little boy and his mother say they'll never forget witnessing the cruelty of one agent to a little girl whom they ran into in their agent's office. "This boy is prettier than you are and you're as tall as he is," the agent pointed out to the girl, saying the agency didn't want her. "Come back when you're prettier and you've stopped growing." Kelman claims a diplomatic tack is best. "If we don't want a child, we try to be very tactful. I tell the mother she has an adorable youngster but he's not ready for the business. We try to do it without putting the child down."

"Give them that smile and they'll *have* to hire you," Evelyn Schultz coaches her clients. "I encourage them to have fun."

Fun is really not the most accurate word. An agent's orders can be confusing. Be aggressive, but not too pushy. Don't worry about losing, but by all means get the part. Relax at the interview, but beat out the competition.

Agents may talk about kids in the business having fun, but their foremost concern is doing good business. One manager admitted to me that when a client failed to land a part in a series that they were all counting on, she called him up to scold, "You blew it! One man didn't like you!" She explains her harsh attitude by saying, "I don't believe in playing. It's too painful to lose. It's hard on the mother, especially if she drives an hour and a half to get to the interview."

Hollywood agents can generally be described as experts in many things other than the application of tact. I will never forget how angry my agent became when I cut my waist-length hair. I was thirteen years old, weighed less than sixty pounds, and looked ridiculously juvenile to be in junior high school. Kids my age teased me by asking if I had sneaked onto the junior high grounds from the elementary school next door. I figured fewer inches of hair might add a few more notches of sophistication to my look. But when I walked into his office with my new chin-length coif, my agent erupted like Mount Saint Helens. Having had steady success peddling me as the appealing long-haired waif, he took one look at my pageboy cut and saw his own income trimmed. "Didn't I tell you to keep your hair?" he screamed at me. After an awkward silence, he composed himself by saying, "Well, we're selling you, not your hair." My mother, who had originally opposed the new cut, was now worried that the agent would drop me entirely. He didn't.

Agents will rarely try to level with mothers, because after a few words of criticism they're hustling their kids to new agents. Agent-hopping is a favorite pastime. If a child is not picking up work, the mother blames the agent. If parts that are good but not great are coming the child's way, the agent must be the reason they're not better. An ambitious mother is guided by the undying belief that the right agent can launch her child into the right constellation of stars, no matter how limited his talents. "Parents call me and say, 'My kid didn't get the part, what's wrong with him?' " says Toni Kelman. "I tell them, 'Maybe they just want to buy a red glass today. If you're a yellow glass, you're not going to get picked.' Or I use a different shape glass to illustrate." But some mothers will always see the glass, no matter how large, as half empty. "I fired one mother in the middle of the night," says agent Don Schwartz. "I had gotten the kid twenty-five commercials in one year, but his mother called me to say she wanted him starring in the movies." Manager Tami Lynn wails, "I have a client who's Mexican and his mother wants him to go out on all-American calls."

Particularly ambitious mothers may on the sly do business with two agents at once, so as to double their children's chances and not miss out on any important interviews. Agents refer disparagingly to the process as double-agenting; the mothers usually get caught in the act. They are so maladept at clandestine operations! "A girl was interviewed here who had pictures with four or five other agents' logos papered over during the space of one year's time!" agent Joy Stevenson told me. "Two other agents warned us, 'Watch it, she bounces!' " But to give bouncy mothers the benefit of the doubt, it must be said that in general, loyalty to an agent does not pay. A child who stays with one agent over a period of ten years will be less enthusiastically promoted than the agency newcomer who happens to be hot. To be sure, agents can get burned, too. "I have built up several kids from the start of their careers to the point at which they become names," says Toni Kelman. "Then they leave. I resent not being able to cash in on all the hard work we've done—on the really big money." Children who become stars want agents who are stars. If they are famous or established enough, they will likely progress to adult agents. This rite of passage is a high honor, because it means the adult agent considers your star quality and moneymaking capabilities on a par with that of his adult stars—no small accomplishment for a Hollywood child! Only the brightest child stars, however—such as Ricky Schroder and Danielle Briseboise (*Archie Bunker's Place*, 1978–1983)—merit the attentions of the William Morrises of the business. "I left my children's agent when I did *Goodbye Girl*," says Quinn Cummings. "There comes a time when you have to leave a children's agent. Mine didn't know how to handle a child doing a lead in a very big picture. Two days after my nomination for an Academy Award, I was sent on an interview for a commercial. It wasn't appropriate!"

The assertive Hollywood kid may be wise beyond his years. Whenever I would hear of an interview that I hadn't been sent out on, I would cry, or sit in my room and write notes about how I wanted to tear my agent's eyes and ears out. Tired of my complaints (not to mention my crazed, Dostoyevskian crayon doodlings), my mother would schedule appointments with potential new agents.

I was relatively stable. I had only five agents during my six-year-long career, an unusually low figure among child actors. In truth, I hated the ordeal of switching. The exit was always a difficult scene; choosing the new agent was nerve-wracking. First, you had to eliminate the agent who represented your top competitors. Another one would be ruled out because she had a surplus of kids in your ethnic or age category. And you had to beware of the agent who would promise you everything; that was the type most likely to double-cross you. She would fawn all over you and your mother, raving about your adorable outfits, praising your terrific talent, saying over and over that you were her number one client; and then hustle a script in advance of an interview to another kid.

Taken as a whole, agents were a major reason why the acting world helped make me cynical and distrustful of people at an early age, traits that have endured, alas, to this day. "I always hated my agents," Darryl Hickman told me. "They were silver-tongued. They would charm and flatter me while my mother was constantly fighting with them about everything—money, billing, contracts. . . ." My own experience with agents was generally bitter—but nothing very unusual for a Hollywood child.

four

School Days

Around the age of six, the would-be Hollywood child actor is thought ready for some fixing up. Making the talent more versatile makes the child more marketable. With the supply of hopefuls growing year by year, the child must be groomed, beautified, trained and coached to keep him employable. Or so it is said. Hundreds of kids will be gunning for every job. Rejection, even repeated, is routine. "We accepted as a client a six-year-old girl who went out on thirty-nine interviews and thirty-six callbacks without getting a job," one agent told me. "But we loved and believed in her. Now she's seven, and she's done thirteen commercials."

Did her luck just change? Or did she, in effect, manufacture her own improvement in fortune by perseverance and hard work? Most Hollywood mothers and agents hold firmly to the belief that "when preparation meets opportunity, that's success," in the words of one mother who began prepping her four-year-old daughter by showcasing her in beauty and talent pageants at age two and a half.

In Hollywood, the cost of training a mere child can represent a substantial investment, but like the title character in Broadway's *Annie*, parents will bet their bottom dollar on tomorrow. No price is too high to pay for success. Is it a cost-effective instrument? "If the kid makes it," one agent told me, "it's all a tax deduction." Perhaps, but Hollywood's virtually axiomatic belief in the necessity of professional schooling needs to be examined carefully. A lot of what passes for serious child-actor training is, in fact, a colossal waste of time and money.

History can unquestionably be shown to support the pro-child-trainers. In the past, Hollywood child performers were for the most part manufactured, not born. Proper preparation was considered essential. Prior to the advent of television commercials, which require a right look more than training and talent, the demands on professional children were rigorous.

In the old days of the movies, Ethel Meglin, the famous pioneer teacher, put together a nationwide chain of schools that offered a kind of all-purpose training in singing and dancing. The quality of her graduates was legendary. The original crop of Meglin kiddie grads included Judy Garland, Jane Withers and Shirley Temple. Their successes focused a great deal of national attention on the school, and Ethel Meglin's fortune was made.

In the thirties and forties, the luckiest parents were relieved of the financial burden of priming their children by the major studios. Those under contract, like Judy Garland, Deanna Durbin and Mickey Rooney, benefitted from excellent instruction available in the entertainment industry. They were tutored by resident MGM drama teachers, voice teachers, and dialogue coaches who taught them general techniques and coached them for specific roles in MGM films.

Other big studios, like Paramount, offered topnotch training in some of the most minute aspects of film acting. "They learned how to sit, walk, dress, act," remembers Paramount's former resident schoolteacher Catherine Deeney. "Every afternoon, the kids would go to the studio drama teacher. There were two resident voice coaches teaching accents, and there was an overall talent director."

Such elaborate efforts would be clearly excessive for many jobs today. "For commercials, you can get by being just a cute little kid," explains Hollywood agent Toni Kelman. "A lot of my little kids will never do other types of studio work. They cannot do a sustained scene. But they can do what's called for in a commercial. Because it's a very short shot. The child just runs in and says something like 'Hi, Mommy,' and then the camera cuts to the mother."

You don't have to be Margaret O'Brien for a dog food commercial. But many children, not to mention parents, entertain greater dreams in their hearts than an Alpo spot. Hard work makes sense to them. They know it is a serious business, and an intimidating one. Incontestably, a knowledge of professional technique can help a shy child dance out from under his mother's skirts. Simply by grasping the acting, singing or dancing teacher's hand, the child can be guided toward the bright lights.

At nine-thirty on a clear, sunny Sunday morning in Hollywood, 200 parents and children show up for a six-hour seminar. The topic is "Children in Commercials—a Guide to Parents," but, for once, the parents are the center of attention. The show of information and advice is pitched to them.

Many opt to bring the kids along. (Admission for adults costs thirty-five dollars; one child can be admitted for free, with each additional one costing only ten dollars.) You never know! Exposure, as well as information, may be gained. The seminar speakers are agents, casting directors, photographers and directors who are constantly on the lookout for new talent.

The seminar begins on the subject of training. "Acting lessons will cost a couple of hundred dollars," explains panelist and supermom Dolores Jacoby.[1] "But one commercial pays $300

---

[1] Dolores Jacoby, whom you have read about in other chapters, is the mother of five highly successful child actors.

a day. You can get residuals up to $25,000. (The cost of a class) is like putting money into a business." She cautions parents never to lose heart. "Not all children are outgoing," she says. "Mine weren't. Now they don't shut up. This can take about a year."

The dangers of rip-offs are discussed. Parents are warned about photographers who lure mothers into spending absurd amounts of money, up to $2500 in one notable instance, on a single set of pictures. Mothers of infants are particularly easy targets, agent Jeanette Walton of the Wormser, Heldfond & Joseph Agency explains. "One mother spent nine hundred dollars on a nine-month-old child's photos. I screamed, 'You know that child is going to change fast and need new ones!' "

Agent Evelyn Schultz of WHJ advises the parents to present favorable pictures of *themselves.* "On interviews, be aware that the casting person is watching you, the parent, as well as the kid outside. So don't fuss or nudge." Continues casting director Sharon McGee, of the Los Angeles-based firm Chambers and Associates, which produces TV commercials (clients have included Duncan Hines and McDonald's), "The role of the parent in the waiting room is not to hob-nob, but to help your child get the part." The dialogue in the script, parents are warned, is more important than the dialogue going on in the waiting room.

Both children and adults in the audience pop up with questions. "I have braces," says one ten-year-old girl. "Will that keep me from getting parts?" Agent Ruth Hansen of Toni Kelman & Associates minces no words. "Almost out of the business," she says. The child looks hurt.

A mother wonders whether she should change the last names of her seven adopted Latin children. Would that enhance their marketability? "I saw a little girl in a play who was wonderful," answers Hansen, who announces herself as a firm believer in creative name-makeover. "Her last name was Rosetti. She was not ethnic looking. But when casting directors would hear that name from an agent, they'd say, 'Don't bother!' So we changed her name and now she goes out on almost all kinds of calls." Agrees agent/panelist Harry Gold, (the father of Missy, Tracey, and Brandy): "In my range of experience, an ethnic name is not a good idea." His own real name, he confesses, is Goldstein. "Our girls don't look ethnic anyways," he says. "Still, don't give anyone any reason to exclude you. They look for things like that."

No hazard in the business is insurmountable (except perhaps braces!), the parents are told. "If you have fortitude and determination, you'll get there," Jacoby promises. Regaling them with the economic plums of success, she reveals that two of her children financed college with payments from residuals for commercials. Then agent Jeanette Walton says, "I always interview new faces. That's the crux of our business. *Those few who make it big could be yours.*" Not surprisingly, this is the most enthusiastically applauded statement of the seminar.

A parent asks, "But do children love the business as much as their parents?"

"Me and my sister Tracey do acting just for fun," offers a reflective Missy Gold, also on the panel. "But there are a lot of kids who act out there and they hate it." And that, the moderator suggests in her closing speech, could be tragic. "Little kids should be allowed to be little kids," she warns. "You as parents should try not to push them. Because if they're not having fun, they'll all be in psychiatrists' offices later on. Like we are."

For Dolores Jacoby, this seminar, held in January 1982, initiated a promising change in her own career. Shortly thereafter, she embarked on a southern California lecture circuit. As the banner headline on her press release put it: WINNING STAGE MOM DOLORES JACOBY SHARES HER SUCCESS STORY WITH INTERESTED PARENTS THROUGHOUT SOUTHERN CALIFORNIA. For twenty-five dollars, Hollywood's mothers and fathers coddling Hollywood's stars of the future can pick up such pointers as: how she got each child started; what the benefits of acting are for both children and families; how she creates a constructive, non-competitive atmosphere among her five acting children; and how she juggles a self-proclaimed "healthy" combination of social activities, career and school work in her children's lives. To demonstrate her prowess in the business, each lecture comes complete with a slide presentation of stills of her various children at work. To beat the drums for her act, Jacoby took out an advertisement in the *Los Angeles Times*, featuring a photograph of a broadly smiling Billy Jacoby, thirteen, above a caption that read: "This kid earns THOUSANDS . . . doing something he loves." The ad beckoned, "Kids are earning $5000 to $150,000 a year in TV, film and commercials. Come and listen. YOUR CHILD COULD BENEFIT. . . ."

Things soon snowballed. With the help of the Los Angeles Actors' Exchange, which was cut in on the deal, Jacoby put together a three-stage program of seminars designed to educate both parents and children. The seminars, which could be taken either individually or as a complete interrelated course, included:

Stage One: "Scratching the Surface"—the do's and don'ts of getting started.

Stage Two: "Getting Set"—how to go about getting those first jobs.

Stage Three: "Taking Action"—a weekend workshop designed to instruct both children and parents using a variety of techniques, including, in fact, a special simulated audition.

Promising fun times as well as rewards, the program's highlight for the weekend was a special panel of celebrity children "from your favorite TV movies and show." The underlying pitch to the lesson plan: perhaps these children's successes will rub off on your own. Jacoby's vision is expansive. "My dream is to have a summer camp for kids where they can study acting and parents can get counseling too," she said in February 1982. In the summer of that year, she celebrated the opening of the first day camp offering two-week-long sessions for children and parents who want to make it in Hollywood. Within five weeks of the course announcement, they were virtually booked up.

You could hear the shrill command from the office behind the waiting room.

"Say, 'I like ice cream!' "

"I like ice cream!" echoes the shrill voice of a little boy.

"Say, 'Look what I found!' " the woman yells.

"Look what I found!" the boy belts out, his voice cracking under the strain.

The scene is the Hollywood studio of Margo Vann, a longtime professional photographer specializing in the performing artist. Using a host of props under the bright lights and cameras of her inner office, Vann is trying to get the little boy in the right mood for his new set of photographs.

Not to overstate the point, photographs may be the single most crucial element in every child actor's career. Without a good set of shots, the greatest of talents may go underexposed. A portfolio of photographs is a pass without which a child is denied entry into an agent's or manager's office. Pictures must first be submitted by mail before the potential client will be granted a personal interview. Photographs are a child actor's admission ticket to a great many interviews. Some casting directors draw up audition lists solely by reviewing pictures submitted by agents, or by running through the pictures in the children's section of the Academy of Motion Picture Arts and Sciences *Players Directory*. After the initial auditions, they may compose the callbacks by reviewing the stack of pictures accumulated from the first call. Agents, managers and casting directors believe that no future star, not to mention journeyman child actor, can escape the eye of a professional camera; they really believe the camera never lies. "One of the tell-tale signs of a shy (i.e., unemployable) child is the same expression in the photographs," says commercial casting director Elna Lawrence. "I insist on composites." Accordingly, if there is one golden rule to any photographic session, it is to aim for as wide a range of looks as possible. "It's like selling furniture," explains agent Toni Kelman. "If you have the pictures of the living room in different settings, people can see what it's going to look like."

To tell a sad story in full, Hollywood casting directors have a notorious, industry-wide reputation for their lack of imagination. If they interview you once for the part of an Indian, they will always remember you as an Indian. If you've ever made an impression on a TV commercial, you will remain affixed in their commercial brains forevermore as a Kellogg's kid, a spoon glued to your lips. Agents and managers may insist on the need for a variety of poses and costumes in the portfolio on the grounds that the child's marketability is increased; in fact, they are trying to overcome the inherent tunnel vision of most casting directors. "If it's a part for a nurse," says Vann, "you submit a picture with a nurse's uniform. If you're up for a streetwalker part, you won't make it with a sweet college picture."

Agents and photographers collaborate closely to achieve the desired range of effects. "If I see him as Huckleberry Finn, then I want him like Huckleberry Finn," says Los Angeles-based children's manager Jean Page, who regularly spends mornings supervising her clients' photographic sessions. "If I see him Gay Nineties, then I want him like that." Only babies are exempt from the requirement of photographic versatility. Los Angeles photographer Buddy Rosenberg says head shots are about all he takes of his one-and-a-half or two-year-old clients. "They don't like the lights flashing," he says, "so most of the time I just shoot them crying."

A $2500 fortune isn't needed to achieve a good range of looks. Seventy-five dollars should buy an hour of shooting and thirty-six proofs to choose from. Something like $200 purchases six eight-by-ten prints, drawn from a pool of close to three hundred shots and four or five different looks.

The Hollywood photographer has his business down almost to a science. There is no art to knowing the range of stock shots that casting directors are sure to go for. Consider, for example, the child who is interested in serious acting. His pictures should portray:

1. the bratty look
2. the soulful look
3. the happy look

No other look is needed. Except for the ethnic child. For Chicano parts, says Vann, "They want the street look, the gang look, if it's a part for a boy. So you get him looking grubby, wearing a leather jacket." For the Mexican child, however, a different image sells. "You get the farm look," Vann says, "a white peon shirt and wash-and-wear Levis. With girls, you use the peasant blouse, the Carmen-type thing." In Hollywood, there is a stock shot to reinforce every racial stereotype. For the black male child, says agent Jim Bridges, father of Todd Bridges of *Diff'rent Strokes*, "all you need is two poses. Then you can go on a streetwise call one week, an apple pie call the next." For the apple pie look, the child needs only to appear neat, clean, homespun—and above all, nonthreatening. Yes, there is one type of look, captured in one type of shot, that will attract the least resistance. "It is the WASPy, middle-of-the-road, non-committal look to fit any [Caucasian] parent in the world," says photographer Rosenberg.

A range of poses requires a variety of settings. Margo Vann's office is cluttered with as many backdrops—beaches, western towns, the country, baseball diamonds—as most Hollywood studio lots. Props add an additional touch of realism. For beach scenes, those slippery rubber creepy-crawly crabs come in handy; for the all-American soda fountain shot, plastic hamburgers and ice cream. Some Hollywood photographers will have wardrobe racks lined with western bonnets, house-on-the-prairie-style dresses, and Salvation army tatters (for the urchin look).

The only major talent here, besides inserting film into the camera, is manipulating the sometimes unwilling models. "In one picture, I'm holding groceries and wearing glasses for a comedy look," fifteen-year-old Pat Petersen complains scorn-fully. "In another, I'm an orphan standing by a tree, wearing a hat with a piece of straw in my mouth. I don't like to take pictures, because you have to be phony to have these different 'looks.' " The right look requires the right frame of mind, which for some kids means overcoming a serious psychological block. Many a stylish young little actress, accustomed to wearing exclusive dresses carefully hand-picked by Mother, responds to Vann outfitting her in a western-style get-up by bursting into tears. Sessions come to a screaming halt. An unprepared two-year-old child cries out in protest after having bitten into the plastic ice cream cone. This is when the Hollywood studio photographer wishes he'd gone into a quieter line of work, like covering wars. "Some kids are out to get you," says Vann, not joking.

Despite all the effort, only so much illusion can be achieved with a camera. Even the most resourceful photographer in the business will have trouble making Eliza Doolittle into Princess Diana. If you are a very definite type, it is difficult to pose you in all manner of molds. I know from experience. There was very little anyone could do with a sad, wide-eyed, dark and wan-looking ethnic waif like me. But how they tried! My mother would dress me in a sailor blouse, or a Peter Pan-collared dress (always a dark color, to make my skin look comparatively lighter) and hair ribbons to match, none of which ever looked natural on me. My essential look was not, alas, "fresh and breezy," as my photographers used to say. More like one of the Sisters Karamazov, I'd say. I was rarely shot with the happy look. The better photographers in Hollywood knew quickly what my agents and mother only grudgingly came to accept—casting directors would never buy me happy.

Every photographer uses the same standard backdrops and location spots for his very young subjects. This meant that I was required to meld into their backgrounds. But instead of fitting in, I usually stood out. While other kids would be shot smiling sweetly as they stood behind a white picket fence, I would be shot gazing dreamily up at the sky, as if looking off into the Twilight Zone. While others had pictures of themselves playing jacks on the back steps of a house, all I had to do was sit there and I automatically looked like an ad for welfare housing or a potential poster girl for the United Nation Children's

Relief Fund. It was all as awkward for me as biting into a plastic ice cream cone.

As I entered my teen years, my agent made several last, well-intentioned stabs at trying to move me away from the well-known waif image toward that of a more conventional (and more readily saleable) young actress. Perhaps the onset of adolescence raised new hope after so many years of typecasting. Perhaps I could be made over into a new type to cast. The assumption, of course, was wrong, and I could have told them that. I resented those awkward sessions during which I was made to pose with such conventional commercial props as a transistor radio (which I never owned); a tennis racket (which I have never swung); and even a tree (which I'd never climb—I'd never be able to get down!).

Heroically, top glamour photographer Harry Langdon, later famed for his work with sex symbols like Morgan Fairchild and Victoria Principal, but only a fledgling artist when we approached him in the early sixties, accepted mission impossible—trying to make Andrea Darvi look more "commercial." My mother and I had gone to discuss my potential at his studio on the main *nouveau riche* drag of the North Valley in Los Angeles, where he showed us books of his work. We flipped through page after page of big-bosomed bikini beauties. I was envious and almost inclined to give it a try, but my mother was embarrassed by the implicit suggestion that commercials weren't the only way to go. My mother was no Teri Shields, I was no Brooke, and Langdon was a gentleman who was quite prepared to accept my mother's request for innocent commercial poses *only*.

Langdon gave it his best shots—of me riding a bicycle, drinking Pepsi, posing outside a restaurant pointing to a Carte Blanche decal, modeling a miniskirt in front of a snazzy sixties Corvette. Technically speaking, these were the finest set of photographs I had ever had taken. But they were incapable of enhancing my value in the commercial marketplace by trying to make me look like Christie Brinkley when I was more like a little Rita Moreno. They were also the last set of that type that were taken. At thirteen, I decided there were to be no more assaults on my sense of identity. Hollywood may have had a problem with my image, but I had begun to accept myself for what I was.

For the right pictures, they say you need the right look. The right look requires careful preparation. Creative grooming can enhance your range of looks. Hairstyling is important. Long dark hair is ethnic; curled hair is sweet and innocent; ponytails are tomboyish. The right sweep of the hairbrush may add the perfect finishing touch to the image.

TEETH! "I advise all of my mothers, 'If you see those teeth coming in crooked, get your child to an orthodontist immediately!' " says one Hollywood children's manager.

There may be money in molars; the financial gains of a child's career can be directly related to the quality of his teeth. Commercial companies promoting food and drink products will not look at a child with a less than perfect smile. But since the standards for teeth tend to be so cuttingly severe, ways to work around them have been devised. "We have a fantastic dentist who covers a multitude of sins," explains agent Evelyn Schultz. "I think he does every kid in the business now."

She was talking about none other than Dr. Robert R. Smith, D.D.S., Hollywood's most famous children's dentist. A cosmetic pediatric expert on teeth, this man of considerable personal flair prefers to describe himself as a master in "special effects." Someday, the Academy may well award him an Oscar.

The most special of his effects is his "flippers"—artificial, removable teeth, made of hard acrylic, that can be placed inside of the mouth to cover over crooked, rotated, or missing teeth. Flippers can be made to overcome the deficiencies of a single tooth or even a multi-tooth disaster area. Parents store their children's flipper set, or sets, at home, so as to be ready for any kind of call. "If a child is going for a toothpaste commercial, he should have perfect teeth," explains Dr. Smith. "But if it is a family-type commercial for Tide soap, they may want something more natural looking."

Prior to the sixties, cosmetic dentistry was performed by more conventional dentists who charged close to a fortune and were not nearly worth the money. Margaret O'Brien had to be coaxed into every painful visit to the dentist by a mother enticing her with the thought that she might run into her favorite actor, Burt Lancaster, in his office. Her braces were removed before she began every movie, then put back on when she was finished filming. In my era, child actors needing orthodonture were restricted to wearing removable retainers over a protracted period of years, since the removable types were only minimally effective. If your teeth were very bad, and only permanent braces would do, you were out of the business. But with a little help from Dr. Smith, today's child actor can enjoy a long-lasting and uninterrupted career.

His business is booming. In one year alone, he serviced eleven clients who were regulars in various TV series. Many TV commercials feature at least one of his patients, especially food commercials showing a group of smiling kids. Dr. Smith's office is like no other dentist's in America. "I told the decorators to make the place look like an MGM movie set," he says. The mirrors in the office are bordered by old-fashioned dressing room bulbs. The seats in the waiting room are fold-out studio chairs. The wall paper is designed with sketches of movie sets. The point is to give the kids a real home away from the set. "Thank God we have wooden floors," says Dr. Smith, "because the kids come over and rehearse all the time. Over the years, I've seen a whole production of *Annie* in here."

Dr. Smith says that flippers, each set of which is personally sculpted, must first be tested before stage use. Do they interfere with the child performer's speech? Do they mar his appearance of naturalness? And flippers must be properly cared for. Routine checkups are a must. Children should wear their flippers for ten-minute trial periods on a daily basis, and stop by for checkups before filmings begin. And it doesn't hurt to have spare pairs of flippers to take with them on jobs shot on location, whether they be in England or Rome, not to mention any of the surrounding suburbs many miles and traffic jams removed from his office in Los Angeles.

"Supposing at ten o'clock you get a call for an interview for four o'clock," Smith hypothesizes. "Supposing the child puts the flippers in and he looks like Count Dracula. Then they [the mothers] call and say the flippers need [emergency] adjusting. Some afternoons I have thirty to forty such adjustments."

"I took my son on a commercial interview and his teeth weren't right, but I said he had flippers," one mother told me. The agent called and said, 'He got the part—but it's for tomorrow!' Within two hours we got the teeth. Dr. Smith is very devoted. After all, he's a theatrical dentist."

The show must go on. Supposing, Smith says, two of his patients are being considered for the same spot on a Colgate commercial. He could design superior flippers for his favorite kid. It is a power he insists he refuses to wield, but nonetheless, he is amused by the thought. "I could determine who gets the jobs," he says.

"We usually do Twinkies the first week," says casting director Sheila Manning, explaining her methodology while busily emptying small bags of popcorn into one large bag. "They're so cute when they get the cream all over their faces."

Cute can mean cash. Popcorn, Twinkies, and a number of other foods kids love are standard props used in Manning's highly regarded class on how to perform in commercials. In the past ten or fifteen years, commercial workshops have sprung up around Hollywood. The teaching techniques are entirely different from those relevant to dramatic work. The child's energy level on commercials must be higher and quicker-starting, and the pacing and overall delivery of lines is markedly more enthusiastic, even exaggerated, in style.

Television commercials have become the first proving ground for struggling child actors. In theory, if you can act in a ninety-second commercial, you might be able to handle a longer spot on a TV episode. With the right look and a semblance of technique, the child in commercials stands a chance of graduating.

Of all the types of training available to the child performer, TV commercial preparation may be most worth the investment. A typical course, costing roughly $200 for a six-week period of lessons, may help the child develop skills that could equip him for a field in which five-figure incomes are routine. These classes are also a kind of glass house where children may be discovered. "They [the casting directors who usually teach the classes] will see the child," explains agent Evelyn Schultz, "so that when I'm talking about the child to them on the phone, with regard to a specific job I'm putting him up for, they already know what he's capable of doing. So I can get him out on interviews a lot easier."

Sheila Manning's commercial workshop in Hollywood is typical of the fare. On the first day of classes—always held on Saturday mornings—children and parents study the dialogue in the scripts of already-aired commercials that she passes out before the lesson begins. Some of the children in the waiting room rehearse their lines with their mothers. Others work by themselves, with clenched fists and eyes determinedly squeezed shut, frantically trying to memorize their lines.

Then she tells them that while performing in a commercial is relatively easy, getting the job is not. How to audition is just as important as how to read lines. As Manning instructs the children when they walk down the hall to the classroom in her studio, "The first thing to do on an interview is sign in, rather than stand around and waste time while your mother's looking for a parking space. Besides, if you can't sign yourself in, it means you're just standing there with your stomach in knots. Also, next week I want you all to know your social security numbers. And those of you with pictures, always bring them in. I want you in the habit of having them on you at all times."

Her course becomes a remarkably detailed six-week dress rehearsal for what awaits the children upon graduation—the hotly contested world of interviews. While the two dozen kids in this class range up to age seventeen, most are years away from puberty. But even some of the youngest girls come all dolled up in highly styled dresses, their hair carefully curled and bedecked with brightly colored bows. They are very meticulously groomed, especially for nine-thirty on a Saturday morning. The mothers have obviously gotten their daughters up shortly after dawn to begin the preparation. But when your children are being seen by a top Los Angeles casting director, they have to look their best.

Mothers are not permitted inside Manning's classroom. "It's the only way the kids have total confidence," she is forced to explain repeatedly to indignant parents. Only when she has shooed them away and locked the door does she take her place in front of the class. "The main reason we give these classes," she tells the children, "is so that you won't ever be scared." After a circle of introductions is made around the room, the first lesson begins. The children are asked to describe their professional experience. Twelve-year-old Martha says that since she started working at the age of two, she can't remember all her credits. She rattles off a few. Seven-year-old Chris can't even remember whether or not he has an agent. He thinks he does.

Whatever their level of achievement, all the children are terribly eager to impress their teacher. "I really want to do commercials," ten-year-old Terry insists. Whether by their own instincts or their parents' repeated hammerings, they know how important it is to convince the casting director of their sheer determination. Anything other than the greatest enthusiasm might be interpreted as disinterest or disaffection—two surefire turnoffs to hiring a child. When seven-year-old Tim talks about doing his food commercial, teacher Manning reminds them of the risks they run in accepting jobs they are not suited for. "What if you have to go on a creamed spinach commercial interview and you hate spinach?" she asks rhetorically. "Don't go. Tell your agent you're allergic to it. Otherwise, the dislike will show on your face. If you go out and get the job, but don't do a good job, you won't get another one. They won't remember *why* they didn't like you."

Eight-year-old Risa doesn't buy the advice and deftly punctures its obvious flaw. "But then you won't get the money for the commercial!" she protests. No easy rebuttal to a remark like this. The children in this class are acutely aware of the monetary gains to be made in commercials, as a hilarious incident that took place a little later showed. A well-known adult character actress was addressing the class as a favor to Manning. She was describing a dreadful prison scene, in which she was forced to eat greasy food with her hands. But she got very little sympathy from her audience. Said a singularly unmoved Tim, "I bet you got a lot of money for it."

The class proceeds to more technical points. Manning teaches the children to "slate." To slate means to stand before a rolling videotape machine at an audition, to clearly and cheerfully state your full name, and then to give out the name of your agent. The slate is usually taken just moments after the child walks into the audition room, and is an important first step on the way to getting the job.

Many children are inept slaters. They swallow their words like chewing gum, can't remember their agents' names, and stare nervously down at their feet while they talk. "Look into the camera like it's your best friend," Manning coaches them. The most devastating mistake that can be made while slating? "Never tell your age if they don't ask," Manning explains. "Suppose they're looking for eight and they think you look eight but you say you're ten. Then they'll always see you as ten. If they ask, though, tell the truth." Ten-year-old Terry questions Manning closely. "Should you tell the truth even if your agent says to lie?" Manning urges them, "Tell the truth, because if you go out one week and say seven, then the next week and say nine, they're going to say, 'This kid lies.' It's so much easier in life to tell the truth. That way, you don't have to remember your lies."

When the slating exercise is over, at the end of the second hour of this three-hour morning class, the children begin work on their scripts. Like many children in America, their reading skills are remarkably poor. Eight-year-old Christy can't pronounce "Aunt Jemima" properly, even after a series of tries. "They're very sensitive about things like that," Manning warns her. "If you can't say the name of the product, you won't get the job." Then she tells everyone in the class to keep trying, that it's better to make a mistake in school than on a real-life interview, when a job and money are at stake.

The children are as overly zealous as they are clumsy. Terry, rehearsing the Towelettes commercial, attempts to attain a level of realism by pretending to be wiping imaginary sweat off his face with an imaginary Towelette. Nice try, but his flair for facial melodrama with the putative product causes him to lose his place in the script. Quickly, Manning offers a remedial tip: do the mime with the one hand, but don't forget to trace the script line by line with the index finger of the other. Then six-year-old Eliot demonstrates his embarassingly complete lack of experience in working with a script. He starts reading his first line, but fails to exclude the name of his character: " 'Kid: I like macaroni,' " he yells out. The roomful of kids erupts into heckling laughter.

With the script reading part of the course completed, the popcorn they have been eyeing all morning is brought out. But the food is not there for fun. Manning tells twelve-year-old Martha to grab a handful of popcorn from the bag, then stand in front of the class and eat it. With her mouth full of food, she is instructed to say, "This is delicious!" Not used to talking with food in her mouth, she complains, "I can't!" A piece of popcorn falls out of the corner of her mouth. What to do? "There's a trick!" says Manning. "Put it to the side of your mouth with your tongue, so that you can talk clearly." This is a marketable skill; many commercials using children do require food-in-the-mouth acrobatics.

When the popcorn performances are over, the children review the videotape. Now, finally allowed to eat, they zestily dig into the bag while the series of commercial script readings and "This is delicious!" segments are replayed. Most of the children, however, seem only mildly interested in watching their performances. They are more interested in eating the popcorn than having to sell it. After all, it *is* delicious.

*   *   *

At class number two the following week, they are discussing image building. "You want to play it thirteen," Manning's friend and assistant, Brooke Bundy, chides thirteen-year-old Maria, who is wearing heavy make-up, nylon stockings, and a chic, tight-fitting, blue and white sailor dress with a matching hat. Bundy, a drama instructor and practicing actress, argues, "I'm sure people tell you all the time that you look like Brooke Shields. But that's not where the money is. The money is at thirteen." Maria protests, "But my manager told me to look older." The instructor is fully aware that some young clients are betrayed by managers who devise a Brooke Shields-strategy in hopes of hitting the multimillion dollar jackpot, when the clients' interests would be better served by a more honest, inch-by-inch development of their careers. The instructor firmly informs Maria that the Brooke look does not go well with commercials.

The morning's first formal exercise involves learning to project personality. "We are just going to talk," says Manning. "The purpose of the exercise is to get you to talk in full sentences and to offer them [the interviewers] more than you're being asked for." The children get up one by one, do their slates, and prepare for a barrage of impromptu inquisitions. Some of them resist responding to orders such as , "Be a dog," "Sing a song," or "Tell a joke." But they are made to feel that there is no place for embarrassment, either in class or on an interview. If they are going to feel shy, or insist on maintaining a sense of personal dignity, then they are in the wrong line of work. When eight-year-old Risa gives a sterling performance as a flea-bitten dog, Manning says she is impressed with her ability to "let go." "I'd hire you in a minute," she says. "Good," Risa answers sharply. She has no taste for baloney. She wants work, not flattery.

The more inhibited the child, the school's theory goes, the wilder the exercises he must be made to endure. This is no mollycoddling kindergarten exercise. Some children are ordered to hop around the room and giggle, or jump up and down with their fingers in their ears and their tongues sticking out. The point of the lessons, Manning says, is to learn that simply making noise is a form of entertaining. Silence is rarely golden; unless you are a professional mime, it won't pay. Talk it up, she says, "Even if they don't ask, talk. What you don't want is dead air. If you're boring, they're going to be bored. The real secret is making them forget it's an interview."

Halfway through the six-week course, Manning seems to feel under the gun to impress the parents and get the idea across to the kids that there is little time for games.

The children, who have become friends, gab animatedly before class. Their teacher, passing out their commercial scripts for the day, snaps them to attention. "I'd hate to think you were on an interview and were paying attention to someone else, rather than studying your script," she scolds them. They have been forewarned many times over that in the classroom, also known as the simulated audition waiting room, undirected yakking is strictly prohibited.

Then, looking accusingly at little six-year-old Eliot, she says firmly, "You didn't get a job because you looked at the ceiling on the interview, and the director was afraid you wouldn't pay attention!" The humiliation their classmate feels is infectious. The kids freeze. The only thing worse than not getting a job is having the failure made public. The classroom is suddenly quiet; the instructor has made it plain that errors in script readings, especially at this late date, are inexcusable. Consider, for example, the children rehearsing a national brand name sandwich spread commercial. To an outside observer, the kids rehearsing might seem sharp; they smile, deliver their lines with appropriate degrees of exuberance, and manufacture acceptable levels of glee.

But something is terribly wrong with their performances. "None of you *ate!*" Manning exclaims. It seems that, while commenting upon the "delicious" taste of the imaginary product, they completely forgot to mimic the acts of chewing and swallowing. "It doesn't say eat!" Cindy protests. "It doesn't have to," Manning scolds. "This is a class in thinking, too."

Now the children are completely confused. Having been schooled to be commercial robots—masters at switching enthusiasm on and off—why should they also be required to demonstrate thinking and reasoning abilities?

In important respects, commercial classes are nothing like ordinary school classes. While student cooperation is encouraged within the public and private school systems, it is anathema in the commercial workshop. Take the case of the six-year-old whose continual mispronunciation of words only prompts his overly helpful classmates to leap to his rescue by screaming out the correct pronunciations. The instructor is not amused. "Are you going to the interview with him, all those of you who helped him?" Manning asks angrily. The kids remain silent, but she continues to reprimand them. "Don't help him," she says firmly. "He has to do it on his own!"

It is the end of the intense two and a half hours, time again for the children to view their performances on the video machine. Terry's tape is replayed, and even though this is the fifth week of class, he is forced anew to watch himself slate his name and, not unhumiliated, announce that he still has no agent. To this, feisty Tim yells out, "How come?" A brutal question, but the kids jump to forlorn Terry's defense, telling Tim to shut up. They know what it's like to go begging for a first agent. They know how much it hurts.

An aura of solemnity pervades the atmosphere of the sixth and final class. After today, the kids know, there will be no more chances to impress the casting director. Instead, they will have to impress their parents—by picking up jobs.

Some children show definite signs of progress. Maria, previously made-up and dressed like a Latin American Brooke Shields, arrives wearing floral print overalls, no make-up, and with her hair in two girlish-looking braids. Her mother proudly presents her made-over daughter to Manning, who showers words of approval upon the girl. Now she is presentable for auditions.

Another sign of progress: Terry, who only last week couldn't find anyone willing to sell him, announces with great pride that he has finally signed with his first agent. Everyone congratulates him. He has made it over the first hurdle.

Others, however, are now hostile. When Risa gives her last stunning performance in class—and she *was* terrific—her teacher commends her. "You'd have gotten that job," she says. "Yeah," counters Risa, "*if* my agent had sent me on the call." Promises, promises. Her agent's neglectful behavior over the past six weeks has gotten the eight-year-old's goat.

When the last pair of children are about to videotape their commercial, eight-year-old Jennifer asks bluntly if they will be allowed to see their tapes before their parents are invited in. Manning gives them an unequivocal, "No." They joke nervously about leaving before their parents arrive, shivering at the mere idea of their mothers and fathers scrutinizing their work. So when the parents file into the studio, the room grows very quiet. "They're terrified," Manning told me in private. "They're afraid of their parents."

And well they should be. This is no half-baked PTA meeting. These parents slink into the classroom, GIs on a *Combat!* set, ready to fire at the first sign of the enemy—who is, of course, all the other adorable little children. For the mothers, as for the children, the class is a dress rehearsal for the real-life interview. They are preparing for a future killing.

As the pack of mothers and a few fathers are shepherded down the hall by their children—some parents carrying infants in their arms or pushing them in strollers—their eyes dart around from rival child to rival child. They are rating their own against the competition. Each mother looks a bit shaken at the sight of all these appealing little faces and the sound of those bright, chirping voices. Each is well aware that any one of these competitors could snatch a job away from her child. One mother, escorted down the hallway by her long blonde pony-tailed daughter, Cindy, stops at the sight of a stack of pictures of all the children inside Manning's private office. With daughter in tow, she ducks in. Picking up the top photo of angelic-looking eight-year-old Jennifer, she remarks to her daughter, "Look how cute she is!" The touch of envy in her voice hits her plain-looking daughter like a smack on the face. She takes a quick, painful glance at Jennifer's picture, forces a slight smile to mask her hurt, tugs her mother's arm and leads her into the class-room.

"What we're going to show you is the first week's tape first, then this week's tapes," Manning tells the parents. "Re-member that, because most kids cringe at the first tape; for many it was their first time in front of a camera."

It is a surprisingly subdued half hour. Whatever parental criticisms may be fired at the children for their inept perform-ances are reserved for more private moments after class. The mothers are anxious to make a favorable (i.e., I'm not a stage mother) impression on Manning. While some of the parents laugh at the other children's mistakes (like the videotape of Chris saying he doesn't know whether or not he has an agent) they are clearly on their better behavior. A few of the parents leave after seeing their own children's presentations, but most are glued to the videotape machine. They want to watch the competition.

Afterwards, a few parents linger to discuss their children's careers with Manning. Terry's mother wants to know, now that she's finally gotten her son an agent, how Manning would estimate his chances of making it. Upon hearing Manning's answer, her face lights up with extraordinary happiness. Says the casting director, *"He's going to work."*

Children who can dance are being used in commercials more and more. Advertisements for soft drinks such as Dr. Pepper, Pepsi and Coke, as well as for an astonishing number of blue jeans brands, call for children who can move gracefully. And with advertisers growing hip to the nationwide health and fit-ness craze, now little gymnasts are in demand.

Besides enhancing athletic skills, dance training helps de-velop the marketable techniques required for musical comedy theater. Dance schools can also provide important exposure, because choreographers frequent the schools scouting for talents within specific age ranges.

One such school in New York is located just a flight above a topless dancers nightclub on Fiftieth Street and Broadway. The Phil Black Studio caters to dancers of all ages (none topless). Children from the ages of seven and up can take lessons in tap, ballet and jazz dancing. (Phil Black's sister is a children's manager; her New York city firm, Top Talent, has roughly 100 clients ranging from infancy to eighteen years of age.) Children under seven, however, are turned away from the school. Only the older ones who have begun to develop more adequate attention spans are welcome.

A good thing; dance teachers rarely pamper children. At the Phil Black Studios, for example, there are no classes reserved exclusively for kids. "The classes are taught at the professional level," says Black, a Broadway nightclub singer, dancer and choreographer. "They have to be able to do what they would be asked to do on a job." He is notoriously stern but highly respected. Here, too, the class is regarded as a dress rehearsal for the job.

I never liked dancing lessons on Saturday afternoons. Well, that's understating it. Compared to acting, dancing was boring. Dance classes stimulated none of the intellectual or emotional drives that acting did. I had no choice, however, but to go. My agents and my mother made it clear to me that in order to succeed in the business, I had to develop as much versatility as I could.

When I had just turned eight years old, the New York City Ballet, due in Los Angeles in a few weeks, was scouting for children to cast in its three zillionth performance of Tchaikovsky's *The Nutcracker Suite*. My mother, even the long shot player, took me to the kiddie call. Outrageous, as usual; hundreds of kids had pulled their ballet shoes out of the closet and traipsed down to the Hollywood theater where auditions were held. Even those with no long-range professional ambitions had shown up for the chance of a lifetime, to be in the spotlight.

I waited through hours of auditions that day. Kid after kid half-stumbled, half-danced through the dance master's routine.

Why I stood out, I don't know; no one was more surprised than I when they chose me. I had even been apathetic about getting the job—I was an actress, not a dancer. What impressed me was seeing my face in a close-up on a television screen, not prancing around with a whole swarm of little kids. Nevertheless, I was hired to dance a minuet with about a half-dozen other kids and the New York city troupe in the opening Christmas party sequence of the ballet.

Like many young hams with a little experience, I was nonchalant about actual performances. Young people on stage, whether in the ballet or on Broadway, tend to be remarkably unintimidated by the enormous crowds before them. "I thought nothing about the thousands of people watching me," twelve-year-old Jennine Babo, who played an orphan in Broadway's *Annie*, told me, marveling at her own insouciance the first time she made her entrance on stage at the age of seven. Kids can be intimidated by a single adult agent, director or parent, but fearless in front of gigantic audiences.

It is difficult, maybe impossible, for a young person on stage to maintain a realistic perspective on what is going on. For that reason, perhaps, being in the spotlight tends to be a disappointing experience. Those moments on stage are like a climax in search of a drama.

The child performer is paradoxically both professional beyond his years and naive. At eight, I was an unseasoned perfectionist. One night, for example, a young ballerina who had been cast as a toy soldier in *The Nutcracker Suite* became ill and was unable to perform. As panic swept through the backstage area, the choreographer who worked with the children asked me to jump in. My mother pleaded with me to welcome the chance to spotlight my talent in a role that could hardly be easier. After all, creaking onto centerstage as a militarized mechanical dummy is not exactly the same thing as carrying the lead in *Swan Lake*. But like most kids, I was terrified of feeling professionally demeaned. I told them that I had not prepared for the toy soldier sequence and wanting no part of it. No one could persuade me to go on. Having been indoctrinated with the proposition that not performing up to par was a heinous crime, I was not about to lower my inviolate standards!

My mother once took me to another balletic kiddies' call when I was ten. The Bolshoi Ballet, visiting from Moscow, was holding an audition for children to perform in a sequence called "Ballet School," which traced the evolution of a dancer from childhood to the professional level. I was again chosen from among roughly 100—or was it 10,000?—little dancers. Perhaps the fact that I am of Russian descent made me look the part. Even by the criteria of the Bolshoi Ballet, dancing talent was only one factor to consider in selecting children to perform. They could see that I was a good actress. While other kids probably had superior turnouts, I had superior stage presence. From all those interviews and acting jobs, I had gained a sense of confidence and poise—knowing how to hold my head high and smile with the required aristocratic presumption. My track record at previous dancing auditions was, in fact, nearly perfect. I aced the call for a ballet dancing part on a TV special— Jack Jones sang "Lollipops and Roses" while I cavorted around like a baby lollipop. And I was hired to dance disco-style on a commercial for Kellogg's Cornflakes around the product's animated mascot Tony the Tiger.

Still, dancing was only a minor sidekick to my career. During one rehearsal, the Bolshoi's Asaf Messerev actually stopped the proceedings to insist that I become a professional adult dancer. The famous Russian ballet master, arms waving in the air, declaimed to all within hearing of my great potential. I answered boldly, "I am an actress." When a Los Angeles newspaper reporter covering the Bolshoi's West Coast swing interviewed me after my selection, I responded with the awesome casualness only a child can muster. Said old pro Darvi, age ten, "It is a *pretty* good honor."

At the age of thirteen, I quit taking dancing lessons altogether. At the point of adolescence, the ballet studios expect you to partake of five and six sessions a week to further your career. Like many child actors, I had no long-range ambitions in the dance field, and I felt I was no longer little or cute enough to be chosen to dance with the ballet companies when they came to town. As for what might be required for some dumb television dance routine, I knew I could always finesse that. In addition, I knew that singing lessons were more important than any dancing course. The child dancer who can't sing is less employable than the child singer who can't dance.

But far less is expected of the child than the adult singer. I first realized this on one of my earliest jobs, when I sang, in French, on *The Dinah Shore Chevy Show* (1956–1963). Everyone in front of the camera was actually French, except for myself, Dinah, and humor columnist Art Buchwald, who had a ridiculous comedic role as a Parisian restaurateur. We worked with a cast that featured Marcel Marceau, dancers from the Paris Opéra, and pop singing star Eddie Constantine. I played a little girl who wanders up to Constantine sitting on a park bench, and sings the words, *Bon Monsieur, est-ce que la terre est ronde?/ Si c'est vrai, oiseau bleu, ou-est-il dans le monde?* ("Good sir, tell me please, is the world really round?/ Tell me where is the bluebird of happiness found?")

I was a little nervous just before the curtain went up. *The Dinah Shore Show* was done before a studio audience, and it was broadcast live. It wasn't the crowd of spectators that unnerved me, but the fear that I would mispronounce the French words, or worse, go blank. When I pushed myself out on stage and sang, my voice reflected the strain. One note actually cracked—on the air! I was deeply humiliated and, as the show ended, I was probably one of the younger children in the world to contemplate suicide. But then my spirits lifted, not to mention my self-esteem. After the final curtain and round of applause, Marcel Marceau, Dinah and Constantine came up to me with congratulations. They said that the unrehearsed, adorable crack in my voice had set just the right mood, and had made the scene. No more thoughts of suicide!

Children are not expected to sing like professionals. I finally accepted this when I went on an interview for an alphabet soup commercial. I was eight at the time. Although I was far too ethnic-looking to be cast as the traditionally all-American Campbell's kid, I did have a good voice, so my agent was willing to gamble on me. One by one, little girl after little girl at the audition belted the alphabet half off-key to a scale played on the piano. When it was my turn, the man playing the piano exclaimed, "My God, this kid sings on tune!" But he was disappointed, not elated. I was dismissed before I got to the letter "p." Hollywood casting directors really feel that a believable kid-next-door type must be untalented. Kids who are picked to sing on commercials are usually as tone deaf as they are *nouveau riche*.

Even if singing on key were required, finding the right singing teacher is difficult. Many of the better ones shy away from working with pre-pubescent children whose tender vocal chords are so easily damaged. They consider it an investment of time and effort that does not often pay off. Vocal coaches, however, who teach what is commonly referred to as "personality singing," are readily available. When I was twelve, the musical director at Disney Studios recommended me to a coach whose most interesting advice was that I turn my head in different directions, according to the notes I wanted to hit. Then the next coach I tried offered a suspiciously simple remedy for the nasal tone to my voice. "Flare your nostrils," she would say at every lesson. Great for the television close-ups! I gave up on coaches. At the age of fifteen, when I was beginning to look like a young adult and knew I would soon be expected to sing like one, I began serious operatic training.

Robert Marks, a ragtime piano-playing child prodigy, formerly the piano player at rehearsals for the Broadway production of *Annie*, is a New York vocal coach. For twenty dollars per half-hour or thirty-five dollars per hour, he offers a private lesson to which there is only one hard-and-fast rule: parents are *not* allowed in. "A kid will never open up with the parent sitting there," says Marks. "Conversely, if he opens up only when the parent is around, that's no good either. He has to learn to do it on his own."

Like Sheila Manning, Marks knows that to survive in this highly competitive field, the child must become unfailingly self-reliant. Another crucial step in the process, according to Marks, is finding the right song. It must be something between "The Good Ship Lollipop," which parents love to hear their kids sing, and the latest punk rock hit, which is what the kids prefer to belt out. It should be sophisticated but not suggestive, child-like but not babyish. Above all, it should be innocuous. "Children can sing about the weather," Marks says, "or songs like 'Pennies from Heaven,' or 'Someday I'm Gonna Fly.' Irving Berlin did great songs for kids." The usual classics fall into this harmless category. On any singing audition involving children, one can almost always hear renditions of "Babyface," "Yankee Doodle Dandy," or "Yessir, That's My Baby."

A vocal coach thinks of himself primarily as a drama coach. "I try to relate the songs to them," says Marks. "I teach lyrics as though they're a monologue." Another vocal coach describes his approach this way, "I teach them to be real, and to go with what they are." What they are not is sometimes as crucial to understand as what they are. "There was only one Shirley Temple," Marks tells his clients, "and she was pretty good."

Girls in the acting field want to be Brooke Shields, despite the condemnation she has earned from movie critics; in singing and dancing, the role model is still Shirley Temple. The children's entertainment field is glutted with eager impersonators. Where pre-adolescent identities are not fully developed, mimicry may be the only way in which a child is able to project a strong personality. And parents eager for the quick return always harbor the hope that what once went over big will do so again. "A lot of kids are coached by their parents to look like Steve Lawrence," Marks says, "or like some Vegas act. The kids all want to be loud, like Liza Minnelli, the most powerful and wonderful. And the parents want their kids to belt songs like 'Tomorrow' and 'New York, New York.' Of course, these things never really come off well."

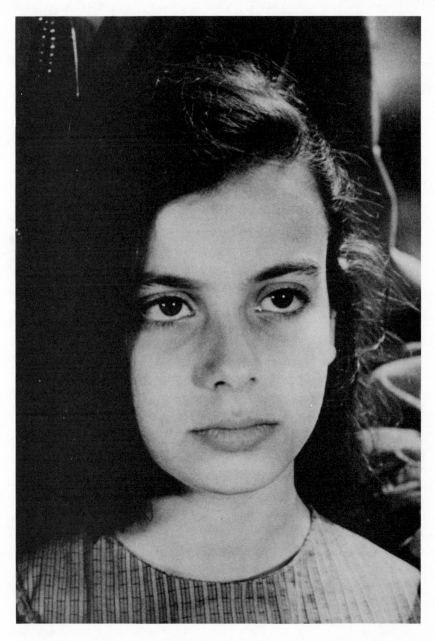

Andrea Darvi in *Combat!* (*Worldvision Enterprises Inc.*)

▲ **Baby Peggy Montgomery (Diana Serra Cary)** *(Courtesy "The Baby Peggy Collection" of Diana Serra Cary)*

▲ Jackie Coogan (*Nickolas Muray, Culver Pictures*)

Our Gang (*Culver Pictures*)

▲ Jackie Cooper, second from left

▲ Bobby Blake, top left; Darla Hood, bottom left

◀ Dickie Moore, second from left; George "Spanky"
McFarland, third from right

Mickey Rooney in *Love Birds (Culver Pictures)* ▶

**Darryl Hickman in *Captain Eddie (Culver*
▼ *Pictures)***

Margaret O'Brien in *The Canterville Ghost* (*Culver Pictures*)

Peggy Ann Garner and Elizabeth Taylor in *Jane Eyre* (*Culver Pictures*)

Natalie Wood (*Culver Pictures*)

▲ Tommy Rettig with Jan Clayton (*Globe Photos*)

**Jon Provost with
Lassie (*Globe Photos*)** ▶

▲ **The Mouseketeers on** *The Mickey Mouse Club*
(*Globe Photos*)

▲ Kevin "Moochie" Corcoran in *The Shaggy Dog* (*Culver Pictures*)

Jerry Mathers (*Globe Photos*) ▲

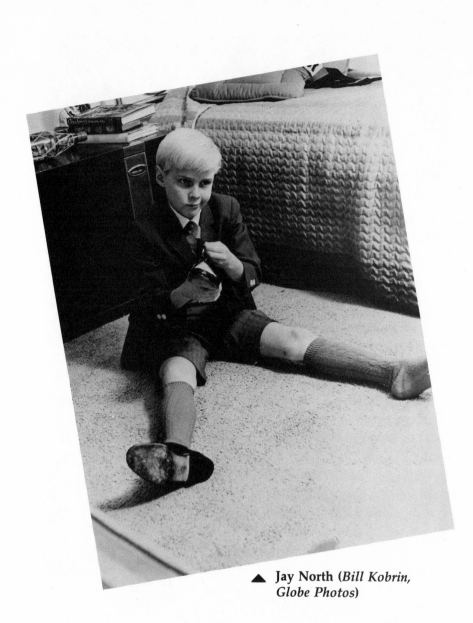

▲ **Jay North** (*Bill Kobrin, Globe Photos*)

▲ Linda Blair (*Nate Cutler, Globe Photos*)

◀ Brooke Shields (*Steve Mills, Globe Photos*)

▲ Kristy McNichol (*Dennis Barna, Globe Photos*)

Quinn Cummings ▲
(*Nate Cutler, Globe Photos*)

▲ Missy and Tracey Gold (*R. Hewett, Globe Photos*)

Andrea Darvi and
Gilbert Roland in
an episode of *Death
Valley Days* (*United
States Borax &
Chemical Corporation*)

Andrea Darvi
with Vic Morrow
in an episode of
Combat! (*World-
vision Enterprises
Inc.*)

Andrea Darvi
with Robert Culp
in an episode of *I
Spy* (*Art Green-
field*)

"To be good is not enough, when you dream of being great." Thus reads the caption on the wall poster that pictures a tragic clown in the mode of *Pagliacci*'s Tonio, clutching his hand over his heart while gazing soulfully at the moon on a starlit night. The poster appears on the wall of the Weist-Barron School in New York City. This well-known school not only offers courses in commercial acting techniques, but also a program of study in dramatic acting for children. Its students start at around five years old and extend to all ages of adulthood. Among New York professionals in the field, it is considered one of the most reputable acting schools.

The Weist-Barron School uses unorthodox methods compared to the run-of-the-mill actors studio. Its teachings are closer to pop psychotherapy than to the classic approaches of Stanislavsky or Strasberg. Children get reassurances; "confidence building," rather than method acting, is the thrust of the first phase of the children's course. Over no less than nine Saturday sessions, the teacher preaches to the kids that the important thing "is to think about being *you*. . . . No one else is like you. Only *you* have these beautiful, wonderful qualities. We build happiness."

But how can inner confidence be taught? The Weist-Barron School has devised several far-out methods. First, there is the Punch and Judy puppet technique. Using hand puppets, two children on the school stage engage in a three-way dialogue with their teacher, who stands off-stage working her own hand puppet. The puppets, then, serve as emotional buffers between the young performers' newly exposed raw nerves and their audience. They learn to loosen up and to express their feelings more freely, by making believe that it is the puppets, not they themselves, who are conversing.

The technique also exploits what the school considers extremely important—the playfulness of childhood—while simultaneously building acting skills. "You have to warn parents that their twelve year olds may in the beginning be acting like four," one faculty member says. The end goal of the exercise, it seems, is for the children to learn to function on their own just like the puppets in their hands, so that when the real-life casting directors pull the strings, they will be able to jump up and down on cue.

There is also a simulated audition designed, the teacher says, to develop a bottomless reserve of conversational skills for interviews. In this exercise, the child and the teacher exchange roles. The child sits behind a desk on the studio stage and pretends to be the average casting director. When the teacher saunters onto the stage, the script calls for the child (now the casting director) to pop the one opening audition question most children loath having to answer, "How are you?"

"Okay," answers the teacher in a flat, dull tone of voice.

Suddenly teacher stops the exercise.

"Now, let's do it again," she says, without explanation.

"How are you doing?" repeats the child, now confused but playing along gamely.

"Great!" the teacher replies.

This is the lesson. "If you say 'Great,' " she tells them, "you make the casting director feel great. And if you start saying those things, you become those things. 'Okay' is not good enough." Go for the gusto of superlatives.

Other elements of the workshop include a certain amount of homework, such as an oral reading program. With a zippy little poster that proclaims "Reading is fun," the child is sent home to read aloud in his room for ten minutes every day as a method of script preparation. Then there are improvisation exercises. The "blue exercise" is one favorite. The children, working in pairs, are instructed to engage in a heated, intense emotional exchange, but using only one word to describe their emotions—"blue." "This is to get you to learn to react and to listen," she says. "Let yourselves go."

After lesson nine, the school holds a mini-graduation. Parents attend, and a children's agent or manager is the standard guest of honor whom the children present with a corsage. The agent then watches the children perform in a variety of scenes from soap operas, plays and commercials, after which she comments upon their work. But the graduation custom calls for the agent not to be too critical. "It's good for the children to see that agents and managers are people," says the teacher.

At the end of the commencement exercise, the teacher presents each child with a "lucky penny" to take with him on auditions, as well as a sheet of typewritten reminders, the last line of which reads, "Have a wonderful time."

It is my own view, as you have surely surmised by now, that most acting schools for children are gimmicky and cost-*inef*-fective. Children, more than adults, tend to be aware and expressive of their gut instincts. Child actors perform not on the basis of highly developed techniques, but on the natural strength of those emotions.

I had a few brief flings with acting teachers. When I was six, I went to the Meglin School in Hollywood. After I flubbed up a Bank of America jingle in my nervousness on my very first audition for a radio commercial, my agent, Lola Moore, decided that the school might help me build up some confidence. I can remember reciting some tongue twisters and rehearsing a variety of wholesome kiddie scenes (probably original Meglin School material) about going to the circus and such. But my mother and I soon concluded that the school was a waste of time, and I learned to act by thinking about my feelings and using my head. My lack of training never kept me, or any of my equally untrained acting competitors for that matter, from getting the good parts.

Certain kinds of specialized training, I concede, can be useful. "Sometimes a mother knows a week in advance that her kid will need an accent," says Los Angeles-based dialect specialist David Alan Stern. "Or, if the kid goes on an interview and they like his look, the casting director may say, 'See whether or not you can pick him up a Southern accent.' "

The child who gets the accent right may get the part as well. Like a graceful, athletic body, a cosmopolitan facility with language styles may give the child a competitive advantage. A variety of dialects and accents are in demand today: Cockney, British, New York, Irish, French and, in particular, Southern. A dialect may be an indispensable element of a specialty role. The finest little actor around town will never be cast in a production of *Oliver* if he is unable to affect a British accent.

Dialect lessons are something of a gamble. You can master the dialect and not get the part, of course. But unlike other kinds of study, dialect or accent lessons are usually only a one- or two-shot deal geared to a specific role that is pending. The child first picks up the dialect by listening to and mimicking the teacher. Then it becomes the mother's job to encourage practice at home. Armed with a training manual and a set of tapes, the mother develops an understanding of the required phonetics of the accent. But valuable as this instruction can be, it sometimes puts a strain on everyone involved. "I don't like stage mothers who push their kids," says Stern. Or the teacher may wind up despising the kids themselves. "Their attention span is too short," he complains. "I dislike sitting with them while they bounce around and look at the walls. It's a hell of a lot harder to work with them."

Not only does Stern offer no junior discount, he charges children an additional ten dollars for each lesson (making a grand total of forty-five dollars per hour). Even at that price, Stern refuses to teach anyone under the age of eleven. "Once they are socialized outside of the family," he says, "when they have been to high school or junior high and can make intelligent analyses, you can deal with them as adults. But while the decisions are made with Mommy, I feel that I am performing more for Mommy than for the child." He is.

I became a master at broken English. I was rarely cast in a part for which some dialect or accent was not a requirement of the job. I learned to speak carefully studied dialects such as French, Italian, Spanish, even British Indian. With my good ear, I was an excellent mimic. I could pick up a dialect just by watching television and going to the movies.

The rare roles requiring normal spoken English were often hilariously memorable. Back in the early sixties, Hollywood's racial and ethnic stereotypes were even more odious than they are today. They were also more inconsistent. Once, I was required to wear an old-fashioned Hawaiian muumuu on the

Hawaiian Eye television series (1959–1963), but I was astonished to discover that they would allow me to speak in plain old American English. And, as a half-breed Shoshone Indian on *Bonanza,* (1959–1973), I wasn't asked to manufacture some phony, primitive "Me Tarzan, You Jane" pattern of speech—the usual Hollywood formula for Indians.

For the non-English roles, I did the best I could. Foreign language study wasn't offered in my North Hollywood elementary school. I knew nothing of the languages in which I had to learn to speak as if fluent before the camera. Sometimes I worked with coaches. As a Spanish child from a foster home in the famous daytime series *A Day in Court* (1958–1965), my coach was a Spanish actor who worked as a substitute teacher at my elementary school but taught me after hours. For the French roles, my mother coached. She had studied French in school. Sometimes at interviews, after an initial chitchat with me alone, the producers or casting directors would invite her into their offices, where they would hand her the script with the French lines. She would read the lines aloud and I would repeat them after her, just to prove to them that I could perform the necessary tricks.

Imitating the sounds came much more easily than memorizing them. Everytime I had a French-speaking part, for several hours a day my mother would take me behind the closed doors of my bedroom and, script in hand, drill me on the phonetics. For the French words, *Nous sommes Américains* ("We are Americans") she would write out something like, "Noo sumz A-merrr-eee-cann."

The pressure was tremendous. I was terrified of going blank on the set, as I had on my first Spanish dialect part. The disaster occurred while filming an episode of *Pete and Gladys* (1960–1962), in which I played the daughter of the Mexican gardener. I couldn't get the Spanish words right, so the director gave almost all of my lines to the little boy playing my brother, who was a genuine Mexican-American. Such humiliation at the age of eight! After that mishap, from the moment when my mother would write out the phonetics to the first day of filming, I frantically and ceaselessly turned them over and over in my mind. I woke up with them on the tip of my tongue, and dropped off to sleep still mouthing the sounds in the dark. On many Saturday afternoons in North Hollywood in the early sixties, you might have seen this crazy little girl pacing up and down the streets, trying to keep the neighbors watering their lawns from noticing that she was softly muttering the words of some mysterious unknown language. Determined to spin them around in my mouth and mind until doing them correctly became automatic, I could then begin to deal with the emotions. I had to be aware of what words to emphasize, where in a line it made sense to cry, or where to simply catch my throat to display a tinge of emotion. I was a perfectionist, and I worked hard. Sometimes I found myself wishing I had been cast in a smaller part with fewer lines. But not for long. Like every other child in the business, I wanted to be a star.

A mother wants to make you one, too. She is always there—after school, after dinner, before bed—to hammer your lines into you. Margaret O'Brien says that until she was old enough to communicate on a fairly sophisticated level with her directors, her mother coached her to develop the correct style with which to deliver the lines. Similarly, Shirley Temple's former private tutor remembers how "Shirley's mother would go over her lines with her every night before she went to sleep."

The child series star today may have his own on-the-set dialogue coach. Bobby Hoffman, who once worked as a coach before becoming a well-known casting director at Paramount, remembers how the work used to drive him crazy. "To cope, I'd invent ways to entertain the kids between scenes," he recalls. "I'd write them songs. Once, a really obnoxious four year old was getting to me. He kicked me in the shins, and he wouldn't rehearse." Hoffman says he once refused the offer to be Gary Coleman's dialogue coach on *Diff'rent Strokes*. "He has his own way of doing things," he told me. "He's not directable." Hoffman gets no kick out of some parts of this business.

In today's Hollywood, the overly trained child performer may be more undesirable than the underdeveloped one. "Very frequently, they ask for a fresh face, naturalness, total innocence," says longtime former children's agent Dorothy Day Otis, "especially when they want someone very young—when they're buying the child because he's a child." In fact, it is the amateur child who is being sought after in Hollywood. With increasing frequency, casting directors are putting out requests for "a newcomer," or "a kid off the street."

"I prefer kids who are relatively *untrained*," movie director Richard Donner (*The Omen*, 1976; *Superman*, 1978; *The Toy*, 1982) says flatly. But every year, parents shell out thousands upon thousands of dollars in hopes of nurturing their children's careers. Are they doing more harm than good? How necessary is all the study?

Listen to Mickey Rooney, one of the most famous child stars of all time, and a real survivor in the business. He is an arch-advocate of the theory that children must be trained.

"When I did *The Black Stallion* [1979]," he told me, "I tested with fifty children. But we couldn't find any child actors in Hollywood. They were not prepared. . . . The reservoir had run dry. No one had brought them along. Their individuality and awareness of their personalities was not developed. We had to go to Pueblo, Colorado [to find the right child]."

What we need, Rooney insists, is a return to at least a semblance of the fine training once provided by studios like his very own MGM. Rooney, in fact, has launched his own school, Talentown, USA, in Woodbridge, New Jersey.[1] Its courses range from singing and acrobatics to lyric writing, and are organized on the basis of carefully drawn age categories: young folks, three to five years; children, six to nine years; youths, ten to thirteen years; teens/young adults, fourteen to eighteen years; and adults, nineteen plus years.

The importance of training is a lively topic of debate, with persuasive arguments on both sides. In truth, many highly successful child stars of all eras never took a lesson in their

[1]There is another Rooney Talentown school located in Azusa, California.

lives. "I go by instinct," says Kristy McNichol. "What I do is walk on the set, we rehearse, then we roll the cameras, then we shoot. I can usually shut off and on real quick."

Linda Blair told me, "I never thought twice about what I was doing. It was just God's gift to me." When I asked Linda what she thought of the intensive type of commercial training I had observed, her answer was unequivocally negative. "I don't think it's good. That [kind of training] gets little kids' heads in another time and place. . . . They start thinking of themselves as very special. . . . I wouldn't do it [for my child]," she says. Peggy Ann Garner is similarly wary. "I don't like to see these young people going to bad teachers," she says. "You've got to be awfully careful, in this day and age, if you're going to a class."

Many former child stars feel that if a child has genuine talent, all he needs is on-the-set guidance from reputable professionals. "When you grow up in the business, you learn from the different directors," Margaret O'Brien told me, citing directors Vincent Minnelli, George Cukor and Mervin Leroy as her finest teachers.

Even the Meglin-trained Shirley Temple learned much of her art on the set. "Shirley would learn dance steps through her ears," her former private tutor explained to me. "Once, she had to do a dance with the man called 'Bojangles'—Bill Robinson. While he was dancing, Shirley was looking around the set. Her mother said, 'Look at him.' Shirley said, 'I can hear, mother.' Shirley was a very quick learner." Talent, intelligence and ambition—not extensive artistic training—are the factors to which many former child stars attribute their early success.

Why, then, do so many parents believe in training? "Mothers and fathers often have their own aspirations in mind," says one New York voice teacher, "rather than their children's. So they are willing to spend all this money in hopes that their child will be the next Annie." For many parents, it is a blind, unthinking, and even naive pursuit. They know nothing about the entertainment business. All they know is that they want their children to be stars. They believe that art requires sacrifice, and that talent must be disciplined. That, after all, is how one becomes a lawyer, doctor—and child performer. Their convictions are further reinforced by the boosterism of an enormous array of people who earn their livings from kids with parents like these.

Parents who are banking on costly lessons to make stars of their children are likely to find only their bank accounts undergoing any change. "I have a great preference for the child with the natural gift," says Norman Lear, easily one of the most successful television producers of the seventies (*All in the Family, Maude, Good Times, The Jeffersons, One Day at a Time, Sanford and Son,* etc.). "I have seen too many who are trained and are unable to do things naturally." Says Al Burton of Universal Television, who previously presided over a great number of shows featuring children (*One Day at a Time, The Facts of Life*), "If they act, they're not right. If they've got technique, they're not right. Nobody taught Gary Coleman how to act. Thank God he doesn't know Stanislavsky. Children should be artless."

five

Chance of a Lifetime

It all comes down to those minutes, hours, days or even weeks on the set, where the miracles of Hollywood are made; the months, even years of preparation; all the lessons, the flippers, the photo sessions. This is the payoff, and the challenge. To do one's best, to knock them dead. Not to disappoint Mom, the manager, the agent, the casting director. Not to fail.

In one sense, Hollywood does not ask much of the child on the set. A striking characteristic of the average child actor's role is the generally limited number of emotions required of the performer. In fact, there are predominantly two, laughing and crying. The child is not usually asked for subtle mixes of these emotions, except in the rare lead role. Of the two emotions, crying on command is more difficult for most children than laughing on command. There are probably more parts in Hollywood for happy, well-adjusted children of sunny, well-established families, living in snappy, upbeat family sit-coms. But the advantages for the child actor who can cry on command are clear—more challenging roles, a more respected reputation, better long-range chances. Known criers tend to get the good dramatic parts and certainly the better agents, who find that criers appeal to the casting directors of the soaps, serious movies and TV sit-coms.

In Hollywood, the Established Crier takes his or her place in a tradition that is an important part of the historic repertoire of the successful child actor, whether in the Shirley Temple era, my days in the business, or today. "I was able to cry easily," says Margaret O'Brien. "I was the type of child who could do a big crying scene, then one minute later eat a hot dog and forget the whole thing. Nobody ever told me mean things to get me to cry. My mother would never have allowed that. But there *were* some things they would say to make me cry, like that somebody was stealing my scene. Or they'd say, 'We'll get the make-up man' [to bring the glycerine, or whatever] if I was having a hard time crying. Since that meant I wasn't that good, that I couldn't really cry, then that would make me cry. Imagine, June Allyson crying real tears in a scene but my needing the false ones! It was the competition thing that made me cry, not someone telling me my dog died."

Only in the world of the child actor does great happiness attend the onset of tears. Anyone who can flood the camera's eye is thought of as a highly employable kid. Alternatively, the child who cannot produce tears on command may find his roles limited to a handful of chirpy commercials or sunny walk-ons.

To accuse the child actor of incompetence with tears is like telling a dancer she has no rhythm in her feet. In interviewing eleven-year-old Sydney Penny, I made what in effect was a terribly undiplomatic slip. I asked her about those close-ups in one wonderful, tear-jerking scene between her and Dan Haggerty in the 1982 TV-movie *The Capture of Grizzly Adams*, and whether those were actually her own tears. She answered angrily, "I *was* really crying. It just wasn't heavy enough to run down my cheeks." I once asked eight-year-old Seth Wagerman to describe one of the more embarrassing moments in his long career. The worst, he said, occurred on the set of the TV series *Quincy*

(1976–). "I couldn't cry. I had cried on the interview and for the first few takes. I didn't want to be sad anymore. So the director told the woman who played my mother to put her dress over my face so no one could see I wasn't really crying."

Tom (Tommy) Rettig remembers that when Otto Preminger directed him in the movie *River of No Return* (1954), he would yell and scream at him, "You little shit, give me what I want!" A lot of actors regard Preminger as a tyrant, but oddly Rettig did not hold the incident against him. Rettig points out that Preminger's tyranny produced the desired effect; he cried on cue. "Then Preminger said, 'Print that,' and gave me a big hug and kiss," he recalls. "I learned not just my craft from some directors, but about life."

Rettig's tolerance and self-confidence exceeds that of many more vulnerable child actors. In reality, crying is no joke. It is difficult for most children to summon up tears in the company of cameramen, electricians and stage hands who, disregarding the drama, whistle, chew gum and tell jokes. And heaven help you if the tears do not come right away; the child knows he is holding up a million-dollar production schedule.

"I had one crying scene that was difficult because I'm happy all the time," twelve-year-old David Hollander (the ABC-TV movie *Whale for the Killing*, 1981; *Scavenger Hunt*, 1979) told me. "Usually when I have to cry, my mother talks to me and gets me to think sad. This one time I kept trying, but I couldn't cry. The director came over to me and my mother and asked, 'How are we doing?' That interrupted the mood. My mother would say, 'Give us a few more minutes.' All of a sudden, I knew what I had to do. I ran to my dressing room. I had just bought something I loved: a metal figure of a man. It was wrapped in a velvet bag with tissue paper. I tore the paper open and broke the man, then started to cry. I ran back to the set and couldn't stop crying. They did the scene fast. Afterwards, when they asked me why I suddenly started crying, I told them what I had done. The script girl started crying. Even the cameramen and lighting men were almost crying. The next day, they awarded me with a twenty-five dollar gift certificate to the store where I had bought the figure."

The moments when a child actor cries on the set can be touching. Everyone knows he is drawing on some genuinely painful feeling to produce the waterfall on cue. David Hollander's story reminded me of the time I was eight years old and filming that still famous Christmas episode of *The Twilight Zone* starring Art Carney. Called *Night of the Meek*, the episode saw Andrea Darvi in one of her more familiar reincarnations— the bedraggled street urchin. Carney was the drunken Santa Claus. The opening scene of the show took place outside a saloon. Carney, in full department-store Santa Claus regalia, stumbles onto the street in a drunken stupor. Knee deep in a blanket of snow—TV "snow," of course, as this is a set at CBS Studios in Hollywood—Carney puts his arm around me and asks what I want for Christmas. Shaking like a leaf from the winter's cold (but actually sweating as if in a sauna under the heat of the studio lights and the layers of wool clothing I have to wear), I say to Carney, "Please, Santa, oh please, for Christmas I want a job for my Daddy." We rehearse the scene twice with no problems, but on the third run-through something special and moving happens. Carefully calculating the degree of quiver in my voice and working up a thick layer of mist in my eyes by thinking about my beloved, deceased great-aunt, I do it again. "Please, Santa, oh please for Christmas I want a job for my Daddy." Now Carney is having a problem. He breaks down, and walks off the set. He is sobbing uncontrollably. The shooting stops; the crew is stunned. My embarrassed studio teacher pulls me back to my dressing room, ostensibly to finish some math problems. A half hour goes by. Finally, the director announces that the shooting will resume. Carney walks briskly back onto the set, as if nothing has happened. But I know better, and for the rest of the scene, Art Carney never looks me in the eyes, as if not wanting to acknowledge that I have pierced the nervecenter of his emotions. I take this to mean that my performance has been a strong one. It is only the first week in

December, but already I have gotten the best Christmas present of my life. The script of this *Twilight Zone* episode never resolves the issue of whether or not "my Daddy" gets a job, but I know that in reality I have done well with my own.

I was a natural and proud crier, but sometimes I did not know when to turn it off. Director Richard Donner once had to tell me during a *Combat!* rehearsal, "Save it," referring to the steady stream of tears I was manufacturing. In one scene, I was supposed to be awakening from a nightmare after learning that my father had been shot and killed, crying, "Papa! Papa!" into the dark. It was a terrific part, one of the best of my seven-year-long career. Crying was strictly optional for rehearsals. The main concerns were getting the lighting, dialogue, action and timing right. But I was eager to demonstrate the range of my crying talent every chance I could get. During rehearsal, I sobbingly clutched Pierre Jalbert ("Caje" on the *Combat!* series), the soldier who was supposed to be comforting me, and pressed my face against his unshaven cheeks so forcefully that my skin broke out in a rash. Everyone on the set stood still while the make-up man applied ointment to my face before the actual filming. My skin had been roughed up, but not my pride. I couldn't have been feeling better. It was as if I had been crying out of happiness.

When a child is on the set, no one can relax. In particular, shooting a commercial is a sprint against time. By California law, a child between ages six and eighteen is permitted to work only four hours a day. (Included over the eight-hour workday stretch are a mandatory three hours of tutoring plus one hour for lunch).[1] Especially when the child is the star of the commercial, this may not give the director enough time. Under these conditions, it is the child actor's unscripted behavior that can bring tears to the director's eyes.

---

[1]The high school graduate may work up to eight hours under the supervision of a studio teacher for a maximum of forty-eight hours per week within six days.

"He does everything backwards," explained the distressed mother of a four-year-old boy to director Ross McCanse (of McCanse-Newby Productions, whose clients have included Tomy Toys and Sun Giant Raisins). They were talking on a Hollywood set where a toy commercial was being filmed. McCanse had been unable to get the boy to do anything right. Exasperated by the delays, he figured he might as well take the mother's very odd advice. "Don't smile," McCanse commanded the boy, following her instructions. And sure enough, the four year old smiled! "Look to the right," he'd say and the child's head would turn to the left. By the end of the one-day shoot, the boy knew his part—backwards, but not forwards. "Sometimes I'm amazed at how difficult it is to work with kids," sighs McCanse.

The director of TV commercials may find that proper preparation and pacing of the child helps to make the most of the time available. First, during the early morning "warm-up" period, one of the director's assistants may play with the child to get the right mood going, to get him laughing and energetic enough so that when the camera rolls, it will appear that the product being advertised induces nothing short of bucolic ecstasy. If, after four or five takes, the kid starts to go stale, the director will take on the role of amateur child psychiatrist. "If what the toy the commercial is about isn't fun for them, I might ask, 'What is your favorite toy?' " says Ross McCanse. "Or just before we're ready to roll I'll say. 'Now remember, we're at Magic Mountain [an amusement park in Los Angeles].' Sometimes I ask, 'What do you like to eat?' If lunch is coming up, I might say I'll get them some Big Macs."

No matter how careful the director's preparation, sheer chance may determine how well the job gets done, and whether the shooting is completed on schedule. As Peter Vieira, one of four staff directors of the Los Angeles-based firm Chambers and Associates, that shoots commercials for clients like McDonald's, Duncan Hines and Clorox, put it, "A child is always an unknown commodity." In a commercial, that commodity also wields effective veto power. If the child refuses to eat the peanut butter sandwich, slurp the soup or pop the Coke, the director's job doesn't get done. There are so many different ways to rebel—by not eating, talking, listening. It happens a lot. Experienced commercial companies in fact sometimes protect themselves from disaster by hiring a back-up child for each role. For the flat fee of $300 a day, that child stays on the set, ready to replace the principal child if he acts up in a way that is not called for in the script.

Vieira recalled the case of two kids he directed years ago in a commercial for the dolls Dressie Bessie and Dapper Dan. The simple, one-shot, one-minute commercial went something like this: the six-year-old girl holds her Dressie Bessie doll on her lap while sitting beside the boy holding his Dapper Dan doll. "I love Bessie and he loves Dan, don't you?" she says. The camera pans over to the boy who hugs his doll and smiles, at which point the commercial ends. The scene was so simple they barely had to rehearse, or so it seemed. When Vieira rolled the cameras, the little girl cooed angelically, "I love Bessie and he loves Dan, don't you?" Then the camera panned over to show the boy glowering and shaking his head "no." The six-year-old girl was astonishingly resourceful. She looked back into the camera and exclaimed, "Oh yes he does!" Instead of being angry, the director was ecstatic to be getting such an unexpectedly hilarious commercial. But it had to be redone. The advertising agency executives wouldn't buy it. They felt the boy's sullen look gave the wrong impression of the product, despite the little girl's magnificent ingenuity.

A set can become a kind of psychological combat zone. When the child is pushed, he looks for enemies. The chief one is usually Mother, but he may choose to launch an indirect fight against the director, rather than confronting Mom directly. Instead of a search-and-destroy game, the child plays a version of dominoes, knowing that if he messes up the director's job, Mom will be hurt too.

One TV commercial director recalled the case of the five-year-old boy on his first commercial shoot, whose father, a schoolteacher, had coached him to ask questions whenever he was confused. This turned out to be a serious mistake. The boy was obviously out to get his father by punishing the director. All day long the boy cried, "I don't know how to do this," when it was perfectly clear that he did. The director fell back on the device of opting to film both the back-up kid and the troublesome kid so that (1) when it came time to shoot the final scenes, he could finish the commercial using either one, and (2) the difficult kid would be scared into behaving by the back-up competition. It worked. Every time the back-up kid was put on camera, the other kid suddenly understood how to do the scene. But it was taking more than double the amount of time it should have to get the commercial done. As the day wore on and tempers grew shorter, the director staged a phony scene that he had prearranged with the producer. "You take over!" he yelled, stalking off the set. He was betting that this final manipulation would jar the kid into performing. But the five year old knew a bluff when he saw one. He simply stood in place, staring at the door, waiting for the director to return. The director gave in, but when he returned to the set the studio teacher warned everyone that time was running out, and there was barely enough left for one more take. The director had only one more card to play. Kneeling down before the boy, he grabbed him by the shoulders, looked directly into his eyes, and said in an icy tone of voice, "You do this one scene and you'll never have to see me again." He told the crew to roll the cameras. Everyone on the set held their breath. "Action!" he shouted. The boy did everything perfectly, just the way he could have at the beginning of the day.

A desperate director may turn to the child actor's mother to bail him out. Peter Vieira was enraged when the nine-year-old boy whom he hired for one commercial refused to eat the scrambled eggs and imitation bacon bits. On the interview, the child had repeatedly sworn that he loved these foods, when in fact his breakfast favorite was cereal. The boy had been under pressure from his mother and agent to get the job, and to lie. Now caught in a trap not entirely of his own making, he sat under the lights yelling, "I hate this and I won't eat it!" His irate mother pulled him by the arm and took him outside the studio to give him hell. When he returned to the set, he ate the eggs and bacon as though he hadn't had a meal since birth.

Pre-schoolers are the most difficult to work with. "They fool around and pick their noses," in the inelegant words of one well-known commercial director. Eight-year-old Seth Wagerman, now speaking from the maturity of four years of hindsight, acknowledges that he was a real pain to work with when he was younger. Playing a very young John Travolta in the ABC-TV movie *The Boy in the Plastic Bubble* (1976), Seth was required in one scene to choke on a teddy bear's eye. The prop for the eye was a licorice lifesaver. "I was supposed to spit it out," Seth recalls, "but instead, I chewed the lifesavers because they tasted so good. They had to do the scene over and over. I went through a whole roll. But I was only a baby, after all." Then he laughed, childishly.

Looking back to the filming of *Superman* (1978), director Richard Donner remembers rehearsing the scene in which the very young Superman is discovered in the middle of a field by a midwestern couple (played by Glenn Ford and Phyllis Thaxter). "He doesn't have parents," the prairie wife tells her husband about the creature from Krypton. True to the script, but not to life; the child actor playing the little Superman couldn't bear such a horrible thought. "Yeah, I *do*," he piped up during rehearsals. Run-through after run-through was ruined. Glenn Ford kept pleading with the boy politely not to say anything at all, but it was next to impossible to keep him quiet. "This tiny little thing kept saying over and over, 'Yeah, I do have parents,' " remembers Donner, laughing now that he thinks of it. "He'd say, 'There's my Mommy, there's my Daddy!' " In time, the child got tired, kept quiet, and stopped ruining the scene.

When a part hits a child too close to home, he may begin acting out his real-life problems on stage. "School is the primary area where family conflicts are brought out," explains child psychiatrist Richard Atkins. "The child knows his mother will get too upset if he acts them out at home. So he acts them out at school. It's a complete transference." But in Hollywood, the set may take the place of school. In the spotlight, the child actor can teach the director, the crew, and his mother some lessons. The problems acted out may have nothing whatsoever to do with the atmosphere on the set, not to mention the scripted story. He can seize the opportunity to express himself more freely. He gets a chance to write his own part. One agent, for example, told me about an eight-year-old client who was cast in a Magic Mountain commercial. On the interview, the boy absolutely swore he loved fast, scary rides. His mother had taken him to amusement parks on occasion and he always seemed to enjoy himself. But the morning the commercial was to be filmed, the boy refused to go on the rides, so the back-up child had to be used. The boy was probably expressing a deep-seated need to rebel or to call attention to himself, rather than a terror of the physical demands of the job.

On and around the set, the child actor leads a kind of schizophrenic existence. Says Quinn Cummings, "They expect you to be a professional on the set. But off-camera, you have to go back to being your age. I'm used to acting my age around kids, but then I get around the adult world and something in my mind says, 'Okay, Quinn, it's time for big people, stop being fourteen.' Sometimes it gets a little confusing because I wonder which one is me and which one is the one I put on. I'm not old enough to assume this maturity on a full-time basis. Preferably, I'm fourteen."

I knew what she meant. By the time I was nine or ten, I'd had more roles than many adult actors. And on every set, where there would be a string of fold-out chairs with the names of all the actors painted on their backs, there was never one for me, no matter how major the part. By the age of eleven, when I knew my days as a child actress were almost finished, I had practically given up hope.

Then one day the miracle happened. I was cast in a rare all-American part, on an episode of *Gunsmoke* (1955–1975) titled *Owney Tupper Had a Daughter*. I was the daughter, in the role of the child of the late actor Jay C. Flippen (*Ensign O'Toole*, 1962–1964). A good part—no ragged clothes, no fake dirt slapped onto my face before every scene! Instead, I wore bonnets, rode in western carriages, and was even assigned a hairdresser. The first morning I walked on the set, I began checking things out before starting. Then I noticed an extra chair wedged in between Jim Arness' (Marshall Dillon) and Melbourne Stone's (Doc) chairs. It wasn't that I wanted to show off, or had been spoiled by the superficial values of the entertainment world. I just wanted to be respected as a professional. I wanted to belong. If my acting career made me feel like the odd one out in school, I wanted to be fully accepted on the set. As soon as I saw the chair, I grabbed it. When all those prop men, lighting men, stage hands and actors saw this little girl sitting in a director's chair with the name "Andrea Darvi" on the back, I was in heaven.

Most often, I found being a child on the set frustrating. Growing up in an atmospbere where the most highly paid, highly billed and well-respected people were a lot older than me, I felt shunned and excluded by my working peers, especially when shooting was *not* in progress. I remember how restless I felt lounging around the swimming pool at the Las Vegas Sands Hotel where the cast and crew of the *I Spy* series (1965–1968) were staying. With evening approaching, I knew everyone was about to hit the best clubs and casinos in town. Except me. I had finished four hours on the set and three hours of schooling with the studio teacher in my Sands hotel room. I was really ready for some fun. Before dinner, I pleaded with my mother to gamble on the slot machines closest to the lobby near the door. I couldn't go into the casino, of course, but at least I could watch through the doorway and get a vicarious thrill. My mother hates gambling, but for my sake she agreed to feed the bandit a few nickels. Just as she began pulling on the arm, Robert Culp wandered into the lobby. He looked great—suntanned, smelling of aftershave, dressed in a snazzy white sports jacket. He sat down beside me and struck up a conversation. Though prone toward curtness with his adult colleagues, Culp oozed charm around me. He adored kids, and I adored him. At thirteen, I was probably on the edge of love.

When he asked why I was sitting there all by myself, I pointed to my mother and said, "Just waiting." He looked disdainfully at her pulling the one-armed bandit as if she were some hopeless casino junkie. Then he turned to me, smiled and said good-night.

When we were returning from dinner, I pleaded with my mother to gamble again. A bit irritated, but still feeling sorry for her out-of-place daughter, she agreed to gamble one roll of nickels, no more. I sat in the same chair in the lobby outside the casino while she pulled the arm of the same machine. As it would happen, Culp came by again. He had no idea how hard I had been pushing my mother, of course, and was therefore led to believe that she was a degenerate gambler, entrapping her innocent child in a corrupt adult world. Walking into the casino, he stepped directly up to my mother and reproved her in a deeply disgusted tone, "Still at it, huh?" Bobbing a look of sympathy at me over his shoulder, he stalked off. Poor Mom!

Some of my best friends—famous actors, producers, writers and directors—were adults, of course. I realize now how few relationships I had with children my age. Perhaps that was because I never expected them to understand the range of dramas that overwhelmed my daily life. Returning from a job to the doldrums of school, or to the unemployment line. Worrying that my agent would fail to send me out on an important call. Suffering through the pain of losing a meaty part to someone taller, shorter, younger or more blonde. I was a bit of a Dennis the Menace myself. I looked down my nose at petty indulgences like Girl Scouts and afternoon school sports. In retrospect, I realize that my attitude was one of self-defense, rather than superiority. In fact, I did not belong to my peer group and could not hope to be invited into it. But I hated to admit the reality of my isolation. As my sense of alienation grew, so did my longing for the companionship of others, but the substitutes invariably turned out to be two or three times my age. As I wrote in my diary when I was a fifteen year old lamenting the glory I had lost, "I loved the atmosphere [on the set] so much, the adults, and all that attention."

The intensity that pervades a shooting compresses the ordinary structure of a developing relationship into a foreshortened time frame. Colleagues become friends. Friends become intimates. Recalls Tom Rettig, "Marilyn Monroe stands out in my memory because I spent three months with her filming *River of No Return*, directed by Otto Preminger and filmed on location in Canada. She was either fearful or shy, so she didn't hang out with the adults. But I was no threat. So we hung out together for three months. I was the only other person allowed in her caboose, on her forty-five minute train ride from where she was staying to the filming location. I was one of the few people who got to spend time in her bungalow. I would just knock on the door and ask if Marilyn could come out and play. We would play word games, card games, play with a guitar, run [rehearse] lines or just talk about how we felt. My biggest thrill was when Joe DiMaggio came on location and I got to throw a baseball back and forth with him. Marilyn was a beautiful person who had all these pressures of what she was supposed to be. I can understand some of them because I felt those pressures of the *Lassie* image and what I had to be."

The hardest part of the on-the-set experience is its conclusion. "There is the problem of having much-more-intense-than-real-life relationships that end," says director Mark Rydell. "*Cinderella Liberty* [1974] was cast with the utmost care. I saw many children. It was a very sensitive role that required real skills. I cast a young black boy named Kirk Calloway who in real life was fatherless. He was very sensitive and needing of a parent. Such a relationship developed between him and Jimmy Caan. Jimmy was very paternal to him. But at the end of three months of shooting, Jimmy went his separate way, I went my way, and the boy went back to someplace like Watts. I wonder how much that boy today believes in the sustenance of relationships. There is a natural separation trauma."

Today Calloway, who lives in Los Angeles, is a car sales-
man in his early twenties. "After three months of working
together, you do get attached," he told me. "When we were
filming *Cinderella Liberty* in Seattle, I had just my mother and
no one my age to be with. [He was thirteen.] So me and James
[Caan] were real close. He would take me horseback riding. I
loved boxing, and he taught me the basic moves."

It was a healthier environment than Kirk had known at
home. "When I interviewed with Mark Rydell, I told him about
my neighborhood in mid-L.A.," he remembers. "It was worse
than a ghetto. Every month someone else got shot or killed.
The first few times were terrifying. Then I grew used to it."

He still longs to return to the set. "The memories are nice,"
he says, "so you look for it to happen again."

The reordering of emotions the child must undergo as he
returns to the real world can be traumatic. To make matters
more difficult, the pressure to act like an adult is never eased.
The parting is supposed to be gracious. When it is time to leave,
the child is required to make the final round of the set shaking
hands, coolly accepting congratulations, thanking his employers. But what he really wants to do is sit down and weep like
a baby. He has lost his best friends.

The longer the shooting, the greater the separation anxiety.
Darlene Gillespie remembers the end of the four years of the
Mouseketeer series. "They just said they'd no longer be doing
the show and that no contract options would be picked up
except Annette's [Annette Funicello]. Until then we'd all been
told, 'You're great, wonderful.' Then there was a sudden, total
lack of acceptance. So you think, 'It must be me.' It was mid-
semester, so we just finished school at the studio. I felt like a
person who knew he had lost his job but still had to come in
until the last day when retirement begins. I didn't even get a
gold watch. In that kind of situation, a really young person has
to accept a very old person's philosophy."

With children involved in the production, termination is
probably no easier for adults. "It's a keener pain when you're

dealing with children," says British director Jack Clayton, "because of the father-child feeling that develops." Says Richard Donner, referring to Harvey Stevens, the star of *The Omen* (1976), "I fell in love with little Harvey. We sent presents to him after it was over, just to keep the relationship alive." Donner says Harvey's terrible sadness at the finish left him with paternalistic twinges of guilt. "It traumatized him," he remembers. "He just wanted to come to work the next day. I remember his parents saying to me it wasn't just that he had to go back to school, but that he felt he had found something meaningful." It was Harvey's first acting job. Until then, he had been a reasonably well-adjusted child. Now he had the bug, but did he have a future? Was he already washed up? "Sometimes it scares you," says Donner. "I had to think to myself, 'Have I helped push him into experimenting with a fantasy that may never come true for him again?' " Mark Rydell has doubts that the wounds can ever be healed, saying "If [parental] divorce is injurious to children, acting and the necessarily temporal nature of those relationships are equally injurious."

Child actors fail to appreciate the necessity of the final scene. They want it to last. And few directors care enough to let them down slowly, although there are some notable exceptions. When I asked Kristy McNichol who was the most sensitive person she had worked with on the set, she named Mark Rydell. He directed the first *Family* episode. "He was really caring," she told me, "probably because I was so young."

I especially hated saying goodbye to my directors. Each one became a kind of romantic father figure. Bernie Kowalski (executive producer of *Baretta,* 1975–1978) who directed the *Rawhide* segment I did when I was eleven years old, was one of my favorites. He would place fresh flowers in my dressing room every day. When he came to tell me that we were finished filming, I remember him holding out his hand to me, but I kissed him on the lips. That night I wrote in my diary, "I will miss Bernie. He was one of my favorite directors, although Mommy says they all are."

There was only one director in my six years of acting in Hollywood whom I did not like. He never introduced himself, asked my name, or spoke to me other than to give me a few quick directions. His name was Alfred Hitchcock. The first time I met "Mr. Hitchcock" (as the underlings in the crew—i.e., everyone—referred to him in breathless, timid tones), was at the wardrobe fitting for the part of a German schoolgirl in *Torn Curtain* (1966). I was just about to leave Universal Studios that day and dig into schoolwork at home when the wardrobe woman said that we would have to go to the *Torn Curtain* set; Mr. Hitchcock was insisting on personally approving my uniform. A director doesn't usually get involved in such details, but then again, Hitchcock was no ordinary director. He was an undeniable perfectionist. When we got to the set, he was working at getting a complicated scene between Julie Andrews and Paul Newman just right. So we waited on the fringes of the set behind all the cameras and action. Hitchcock wasn't getting what he wanted; he ordered take after take. We waited nearly an hour. It was four-thirty. My mother protested to the wardrobe woman, but no one was about to intrude on the meticulous Hitchcock routine. "It should be just a few more minutes," she said again and again. No one dared to disturb the maestro. By four-forty-five my mother had had enough. She tapped the Assistant Director on the shoulder and told him we were going to leave. This sparked some action. About three minutes later he got the attention of the massive, balding, white-haired man with a complexion in shocking pink contrast to his dark blue suit lightened by sprinkles of dandruff. Finally, Mr. Hitchcock came over to the edge of the set, stopped about eight feet away from where I had been waiting an hour and a quarter, took one quick look at me and, with the extraordinary triple chin bobbing up and down like a rooster's, finally rendered his verdict, "Yes. That's fine." I had passed muster.

Although I'd worked with a lot of temperamental directors by the age of twelve, none were in Hitchcock's league. His presence made people frightened and tremulous, scattering like leaves as the master blustered. I was sitting in my trailer/dressing room outside the stage door doing my homework a few days later when there was a frantic pounding on the door. It was the Assistant Director, almost out of breath, shouting, "Mr. Hitchcock needs the girl!" The "girl" bolted onto the set. She was in the hospital scene, playing a German schoolgirl visiting her mother, a doctor, who introduces her to the character played by Paul Newman. It was an easy role, and thankfully I needed very little direction. But "Mr. Hitchcock" preferred to spell out in precise terms when I was to close and open the hospital door and exactly how I was to position the violin [that I was supposed to have been practicing] in my hands. When he finished, he asked me slowly, emphatically, almost despairingly, *"Do you understand?"* Clearly, he had even less respect for child actors than he did for adult actors. I realize in retrospect that, since Newman and the German actress playing my mother had been rehearsing while I was being tutored, Hitchcock had arranged everything so that after one or two quick run-throughs, we sped through the scene. Not for Sir Alfred, the calamity of being held up by some tantrum-erupting squirt! A tyrant, maybe; but a smart one.

"Children don't frighten me," says *Annie* director and lyricist Martin Charnin. "A lot of directors are scared of kids because they don't respect them as individuals. So they create a distance by which they become tyrannical. Children love to have a leader. My technique is to become a Pied Piper to them. They trust me and want to please me and do anything I want them to."

Some Pied Pipers in the entertainment industry, nowhere near as scrupulous and respected as director Charnin, abuse their hold over children. The problem may be getting more serious. For the first time in memory, accusations of child actors being sexually harassed have been reported to the Screen Actors Guild. And, says Screen Actors Guild Children's Committee chair, Barrie Howard, there are probably many other incidents that go unreported. While sexual abuses involving children often go undetected in any field, a silent complicity may be characteristic of the entertainment industry. For instance, the mother who puts her child in the business, then finds that the child has been sexually approached by an elder authority figure, may feel guilty, and partially responsible, for the incident. By not speaking up, she is protecting herself as much as her child. The mother may have an additional fear. If she protests, will the child be blacklisted? A confidential hotline on the subject of sexual harassment, set up several years ago by the SAG Moral Abuses Committee, was discontinued for lack of use. During its three-month-long existence only one call was received. "Actors and actresses in general aren't too forthcoming in these situations," Norma Connolly, a member of the committee, once admitted to a newspaper reporter. "They're too afraid of [bad] publicity." And being blacklisted.

Young boys in the entertainment field, for the most part unusually good looking, are obvious targets of homosexual abuse. These violations usually involve a boy between the ages of eight and thirteen whom someone in the crew has touched indiscreetly or hugged in a way that he has never before experienced. However, since such approaches are made not by strangers on the street, after all, but by people known to the child's parents and everyone else among the close-knit crew, the remedy is apparent. If the child threatens to tell his mother, the aggressor is likely to be scared off. The mother simply needs to maintain a rapport with the child so that both will stay informed and aware.

One child performer, now in his thirties and working as an adult actors' agent in Hollywood, told me about an emotionally distressing confrontation he had at the age of eleven that illustrates the danger of not reporting the first trace of sexual exploitation to a parent. "There was a casting director who was married and had a family," he said. "He was real nice to my parents. One day he said he wanted to take me to Griffith Park to show me the observatory, then take me home to meet his wife and kids and dog. He asked if it was okay to take me for the day. My parents said, 'Of course,' because they trusted him totally. He took me to the observatory, then back to his house where there was no wife, kids or dogs. So he proceeded to rape me."

His parents had no idea what happened. "The most horrible thing was that the next day he called again and asked to take me out," he remembers. "I said I was very sick. My parents said, 'You're fine. And he's been so nice to us, you have to go.' So it happened again."

Eventually, the boy's family left Los Angeles and moved back to their home town in Utah. "But he kept calling me throughout the year," he told me. "He would speak very nicely to my parents, then get me on the phone and say obscene things. Sitting there in front of my parents, I'd have to pretend he was asking me how school was.

"After that incident, my whole personality changed. I became very belligerent. What I resented more than anything was that loss of innocence at that very early age. I went back to the fifth grade knowing that those kids would probably never know what I knew."

By comparison, complaints of sexual harassment involving teenage girls are less common. On the whole, they are sophisticated and self-reliant enough to know how to divert unwelcome approaches. To be sure, there are mothers who sexually exploit their daughters in hopes of getting them work. But most are highly responsible, and the wild teenager is not looked up to as a role model by her peers. "I wasn't allowed to do a lot of things that others were, because my mother was more strict," says Margaret O'Brien, who received firm but caring supervision of her adolescent social life from her mother. "As teenagers," she recalls, "some of my contemporaries were kind of wild."

While Hollywood history offers all the tabloid style rumors of sexual advances imaginable, the bulk of today's complaints rarely involve producers and directors. Hollywood higher-ups, says Children's Committee chair Barrie Howard, are for the most part conscientious, and certainly paranoid, about potentially damaging allegations regarding the sexual molestation of minors, not to mention child pornography. Consider the huge flap over the nude pictures that were taken of Brooke Shields when she was ten years old. That sort of negative publicity serves a healthy purpose—to deter errant mothers. Similarly, a lot of people in Hollywood were appalled when ads featuring a photograph of a topless pre-pubescent girl, in a sexually suggestive pose, appeared in the Hollywood trade papers above the caption, "Would you believe I'm only ten?" Hollywood could, but it was not impressed. As Barrie Howard points out, "She got a lot of attention, but no work." *Exactly*.

The problem of sexual harassment has always existed. But children today are much more aware of what is right and what is not than perhaps ever before. Most of their parents are, too.

Very melodramatic film roles for children create problems of their own. While scheduling demands on kids are easier in film work than in commercials, the emotional rigors are much harsher. "If a kid's tired, I'd rather give him the day off," says director Richard Donner. "Everyone screams at me, but why push a kid? He hasn't taken the job entirely on his own accord. I'll tell someone to take the kid to the park, and I'll find something else to shoot. I can't force a child to bring a scene to life."

In theatrical or film work, the director will first choose to improvise with the schedule or the script before throwing the child off the set and looking for a replacement. If several days' worth of shooting have already been invested in the troublesome child, the director risks a huge loss by having to switch to a back-up. But there is another kind of risk involved in making too many accommodations for the child. Too much bending may harm him as much as excessive rigidity.

Where do you draw the line? "You're talking about an emotionally precarious area," commented former child actor Gary Marsh (*Camelot*, 1967; *Go Ask Alice*, 1973). "Your parents don't discipline you because the necessity of the profession is to be relaxed; they don't want an uptight child. And because you're making money, maybe even a great deal, people give you the confidence that you can do anything you want to do. A child who has not been disciplined will enjoy being uncontrolled and smart-mouthed. When a kid in the grocery store grabs a grape, the parent says, 'No!' But for the child actor, those controls are often off. It is important that parents differentiate between the relatively lackadaisical atmosphere on the set and the 'other world.' If they aren't careful, when the kid gets out in the real world, he won't know what rules apply when. A kid on the street can't say, 'Gee Mister, you're ugly,' and get away with it."

Former child actor Ron Howard (*The Andy Griffith Show*, 1960–1968; *Happy Days*, 1974–1980), now a producer-director, told one magazine interviewer that having parents who were staunch disciplinarians saved him from a lot of harm. "I never got mixed up with this star business versus reality," he says. "My folks were really concerned. There was total supervision . . . When I was finished on the set, I was finished, period."

By comparison, Jay North (*Dennis the Menace*, 1959–1963) now believes that his successes went to his head and made a real brat out of the boy. The culprit, in addition to his own preteen vanity, was an aunt who would accompany him to the set. When other children were in an episode, the aunt would insist on special treatment for The Menace. The aunt's pampering shot up to his head, and stayed there. "I did a scene with Herb Anderson [who played The Menace's father in the series] somewhere on location in a tent," says North, "and I remember that when Herb made some constructive criticism I announced, 'I am the star of the show.' Anderson locked himself in the dressing room and told the Assistant Director he wouldn't come out unless I apologized. I did, but that shows how dangerous this kind of thing can be."

There are many obvious examples of the kind of precocity that is raised to the altar of fame on the contemporary child star scene. The American TV-viewing public seems to love the child smart aleck. Unfortunately, the on-the-set values that boost ratings do not necessarily build character off-the-set. When the child's on-screen and off-screen personalities merge, the stereotype of the Hollywood brat becomes an unpleasant reality. That sweet innocent on the screen soon turns into a sour, snippy little adult. On *The Waltons* (1972–1981) set, for example, there was one child who enjoyed shouting profanities, especially when the cameras were rolling. Her motivation? She was conducting a contract dispute. "She wanted to renegotiate her salary," remembers Earl Hamner (creator of the series, today executive producer of *Falcon Crest*, (1982–). "She said she had talked to so-and-so on the series next door and protested that the other girl was making more money. We just told her to deal with her agent on that." What they should have told her was to clean up her act, or get off the set. But sometimes too much money is at stake to discipline a child actor properly.

On the set, I was a model of rectitude. I tried not to cause problems. I loved my work so much that showboating or tantrum throwing off-screen was not in my repertoire.

In the world of the child actor today, however, the more prominent the talent, the looser the controls. Kirk Calloway, who guest starred on an episode of the ABC series *Family* feels that Kristy McNichol treated her tutor on the set most rudely. She was the same studio teacher/child labor representative who had been with Calloway on the set of *Cinderella Liberty*. "I really liked the teacher," he remembers, "but Kristy was arrogant back then. She referred to her as 'that old lady.'

"Kristy used to hop into carts (golf carts, used for transportation around the studios) and drive off," he claims. "I'd say, 'What are you doing?' She'd say, 'Just hop in!' The director would go crazy, screaming, 'Where are they?' "

Says Jerry Mathers, still marveling about the extent to which he was indulged by everyone on the *Leave It to Beaver* set, "It was like a day care center. You had fifty technicians with things to interest a boy, like lights and cameras and all that wiring. Their job depends on your being happy, so they are willing to spend time with you. The make-up man on *Psycho* was also the make-up man on *Beaver*, so I helped him paste little hairs on a skull for the Hitchcock movie. The producers of the show even had a basketball court built for me on the soundstage. I once found some wood on a back lot and started to carve a boat. The drapery man designed the sails. The carpenter did the fiberglass. Three months later, they had built me a beautiful boat that cost two or three thousand dollars."

The work is often more than child's play. "The most exploited workers in the state are unprotected children," former California State Labor Commissioner Patrick Henning said in a news conference in July 1982. Henning's impassioned comments came in the wake of what he aptly adjudged an "obscene tragedy," the deaths of two children and my own former costar Vic Morrow on the set of Steven Spielberg's *Twilight Zone: the movie*.

At 2:30 A.M. on July 23, Morrow, on cue, rushed out of a bamboo hut—part of a mock Vietnamese village built near Saugus, California—carrying two Vietnamese child actors in his arms. Suddenly a helicopter, caught in the fireball of a special effects explosion, spun out of control. The main rotary blade flew off, striking Morrow, six-year-old Renée Chenn and seven-year-old Myca Dinh Le. All three died instantly. In the ensuing litigation, director and coproducer John Landis, as well as two other production executives, were indicted by a grand jury for involuntary manslaughter and fined by a state agency for violating California child labor regulations, including working children during unauthorized hours and exposing them to dangerous explosives.[2]

---

[2]According to Guy Lee of Hollywood's Bessie Loo Agency, specializing in clients from the Asian Pacific, illegal hiring tactics are disturbingly common where Asians are involved. Casting directors circumvent agents by scouting for Asian employees at streetcorners in places like Chinatown in Los Angeles or San Francisco, or small time Asian playhouses, etc., striking deals with sometimes naive parents in their search for just another pretty, exotic child's face.

Almost a year before this scandalous tragedy, a former California State Theatrical permit officer told me, "You always have independent film companies that don't bother to get permits, or the company may not be licensed and may not have a studio teacher present, but things like this don't usually happen." I was suspicious of the optimistic picture she painted, and for good reason. As a child actress, I had first-hand experience with Hollywood's occasional tendency to skirt the law. In 1959, when I was seven years old, I got my one and only off-the-books job. My agent called my mother one morning and told her to report to CBS Studios with me at four that afternoon to film a segment of *The Red Skelton Show* (1951–1971). We did not know it at the time, but my employers were violating California child labor regulations on three counts. A child is not allowed to work after having attended public school, I had no work permit, and there was no studio teacher present. The mother of the other little girl in *The Red Skelton Show*, who knew what was up, kept warning us not to mill around or make any noise. She did not want us to call attention to the fact that there was no studio teacher on the set or that we were working when we shouldn't have been.

This was the only time I worked in violation of the law. I was fortunate in many ways. Twenty years before the fatal *Twilight Zone* accident, Vic Morrow had to lug me in his arms many times while pretending to dodge machine-gun fire in scenes just like the one that ultimately killed him and the two children. But at the time that *Combat!* was a hit series, Hollywood's "special effects war" had not yet been declared. I was never exposed to dangerous stunt work involving explosives. If that kind of risk had been required of me, however, I probably would have taken it. On the Hollywood set, the pressure to complete a scene at the highest possible performance level, and at a rapid pitch, is so great that by necessity the director may become a tyrant, a miniature Mussolini getting the trains to run on time. In this atmosphere, the observance of legal niceties can take a back seat to the production schedule. Even by outfits as well-established as a Warner Brothers/Steven Spielberg production, California child labor laws are sometimes less of a guide to acceptable on-set behavior than annoying obstacles to be somehow circumvented.

Even selected staffers at the state Division of Labor Standards Enforcement (known in the industry more simply as the "Labor Board") can be co-opted into this atmosphere. "They called at five-thirty that evening to be at the job the next morning," one mother told me, whose eight-month-old child had won an audition. There wasn't time to secure a work permit; the procedure, which is an absolute requirement of state law, usually takes at least a day. "The woman at the agency who sent us on the audition knew someone at the Labor Board, so it was prearranged." The parent and eight-month-old child showed up without a work permit, and no studio teacher was present. Even when there is a teacher on the set, there is no guarantee of strict compliance with the law. In hearings before the Assembly Labor Committee and the Senate Industrial Relations Committee of the State of California held in October 1982, Screen Actor's Guild Children's Committee Chair Barrie Howard said, "Since the production company is paying the salary of the Teacher/Labor Law Enforcement Officer, the enforcement tends to be lax."

Another regulation governs the minor's schooling. For the contemporary child actor, studying at school is not supposed to take a back seat to cramming for the part. The Hollywood child is today shuttled back and forth between public school and the studio whenever a job comes along. Bringing schoolbooks and a lesson plan drawn up by his public school teacher, he is mandatorily tutored in his dressing room (usually a trailer) for three hours each working day by a California state studio teacher/child labor representative. No school period on the set may be less than twenty minutes; but the three hour requirement may be satisfied in short, intermittent sessions of this length. The child must maintain a C average or his work permit may be revoked. This system may seem ridiculous, but in fact it tends to work well. My own experience was that the three hours with a tutor were far more educationally productive and satisfying than six to eight hours in a classroom jammed with forty or so other kids.

In all fairness to Hollywood production companies, perhaps the laws are too strictly drawn to seem equitable to all parties concerned. People throughout the industry complain that the regulations make it unnecessarily cumbersome to work with kids. "It is much more difficult to work with children than adults," says Norman Lear. "To get six extra minutes [of shooting time] can be a major expense and aggravation. It is a crime for someone to go by the book so strictly that a child is not permitted to work an extra two minutes to help other people [on the set]. But on balance, these regulations are good for children. The industry just has to suffer with them."

Not always. There are entirely legal ways around them. When Colleen Logan, area administrator for the California State Division of Labor Standards Enforcement, prohibited Linda Blair from undergoing the five-hour make-up sessions required for her role in *The Exorcist* (1973), a major row was set in motion. Director William Friedkin, furious, uprooted the entire production to New York, where child labor regulations are more lax and less vigorously enforced. Similarly, three years later, when by-the-book Logan refused to allow child actress Jodie Foster to do the explicit sex scenes in *Taxi Driver*, director Martin Scorsese uprooted the entire production to New York. Under New York law, children can be permitted to work long hours, even, under certain circumstances, until very early in the morning. New York horror stories travel back to Los Angeles of early-morning-hour nightmare sessions during which parents or directors have thrown cold water on a child's face, or drugged him with stimulants, to keep him awake for the shoot.

Technically, in New York the number of hours the production company believes will be required of the child for the job must be entered on the official work permit supplied by the Society for the Prevention of Cruelty to Children. It is the job of Special Services for Children, a city agency, to approve those permits. But since there is no state representative required on the set to police the ground rules written on the permit, the law is rarely observed. Admits one New York City child actors' manager, "Ninety-nine and nine-tenths per cent of the time nobody goes through this, and children [who are not babies] are never asked for their work permits." But, defending the attitude of New York authorities as more realistic than cynical, she says, "If a kid has the staying power to work eleven to thirteen hours, what's the objection? I have a client of six who has done fifty-eight commercials in eighteen months and has a recurring role on *The Doctors*. She could work forty hours. She's a genius. She never complains. To her, this is a way of life." In addition, because the child will generally be paid for the extra hours, everyone profits by ignoring the rules. As one New York agent remarked, "I make money on their overtime."

The system places a considerable burden on the child. Author Diana Serra Cary once wrote that Darla Hood of "Our Gang" spent half a day shooting a scene requiring her to hang onto the back of a dogcatcher's wagon. Eventually, she passed out from the carbon monoxide fumes. When Mary McDonald became the resident teacher/child labor representative for children under contract to MGM in 1933, she insisted that in any potentially dangerous scene they use the midget working as the child's stand-in, not the child actor, for the dangerous work. Frances Klamt, Shirley Temple's former tutor, protecting her prized pupil during the filming of the movie *The Blue Bird* (1940), warred with members of the crew over the forest scene in which Shirley, getting caught in the middle of a thunderstorm, hides in the trunk of the tree. Lightning strikes, knocking the bark off the front of the tree and exposing little Shirley to the stormy elements. "They had hooked a piece of bark with piano wire to the tree," says Klamt, "and at a given signal it was to fall. I asked them how they were going to keep the piece of bark from falling inside the tree and hitting Shirley. They said that was impossible, but I told them to build a curve in the tree so the bark would be stopped." The studio, less worried about Klamt's temper than imperiling its star in a preventable accident, ordered a ledge built onto the tree.

In contemporary times, the jobs have not gotten easier. Pat Petersen filmed a movie by a lake in upstate New York when it was thirty degrees below zero. In one scene, he had to roll around in the snow wearing neither gloves nor hat. "They bought me a pair of electric (battery-run) socks," he said, "but you can only be so warm in thirty below. And there was a live bear in the scene that they had to keep controlled, which took more time." It was kind of them to supply the battery-run socks. Not all crews are so resourceful, or thoughtful.

"My worst experience was in doing a fast food commercial in Hancock Park," says Quinn Cummings. "It was filmed in a cold morning [in Los Angeles]. Between takes, my mother got the Assistant Director to give me a jacket. The director screamed and insisted that I take 'that goddamned jacket' off."

Only if the child is a big name is he certain to be spared any ordeals. "Brooke's mother could complain about something and it would never happen again," says the woman who was Shields' private tutor during the filming of *The Blue Lagoon* (1980). But many mothers are not so conscientious, or powerful. It is not that they don't love their children; they are afraid if they complain, their kids will develop bad reputations and will get blacklisted around town. Many mothers do indeed give directors a surprising degree of latitude with their kids. "I've known some directors who have dismissed the crew, called it a wrap [the end of filming], and then secretly told everyone to come back in a half hour—without the studio teacher who would forbid it," says commercial director Peter Vieiria. And without the mother voicing the slightest complaint.

"Some mothers would let their kids hang by the eyebrows for the almighty dollar," says Shirley Temple's former tutor. Surely, an exaggeration. But to what degree? The put-up-or-shut-up attitude is indeed common among mothers who are eager for their kids to work; the children themselves know it. Twelve-year-old actor Shane Butterworth told me about filming a bathtub scene for the movie *Exorcist II: The Heretic* (1977),

"Everytime they said 'Cut!' the steam man would come in and shoot steam in my face. The water was all smokey. I was coughing between lines. I had a sister in the scene who was about five. Her mother threw a fit. I think they must have said, 'We'll pay you five hundred dollars more.' Suddenly, her mother was quiet."

six

Children of the Dream Machine

Late one chilly January night in Arleta, California—near North Hollywood—the figure of a fully grown man stood in front of the tall chain-link fence surrounding Vena Avenue Elementary School. The man was later identified as twenty-year-old Trent Lehman. The schoolyard had been the scene of many happy times for Trent. When he was an adorable, impish-looking second-grader, he was cast in the role of Butch in the television series *Nanny and the Professor* (1970–1971), his one and only big break. "He was typecast as Butch," his mother explained after he took his life. "When the series ended, Trent had trouble finding work."

For ten years afterwards, in fact, he had not held down any kind of job, as an actor or otherwise. He found knocking on doors and filling out job applications a painful ordeal, especially after the initial rejections. Subsequent efforts were occasional. Every standard "We're not hiring now' or "Come back in six months" struck him as a personal rebuff on top of those post-Nanny rejections from Hollywood casting directors. It seemed to him incomprehensible to be turned down for a job paying three or four dollars an hour at age twenty, after having raked in some $1100 a week at the age of ten in Hollywood.

Although almost always unemployed after *Nanny and the Professor*, Trent was hardly penniless. When he turned eighteen, he took control of some $36,000 in bonds that had been held for him in trust by his studio. In addition, his mother had used her insights and instincts as a successful real estate agent to make a series of solid investments for him. Still, whatever Trent Lehman possessed as an adult, he owed to the past; perhaps it was precisely because he was living off the past that he began to feel as if he had no future.

At one-forty-five that morning, an old friend, winding up a late Sunday night out, pulled his car into the driveway of his home, which was across the street from Vena Avenue Elementary School. When he got out of the car, he spotted a tableau in front of the school that at first he could not believe. It looked as if someone had taken a leather belt, looped it around his neck, climbed on top of the chain-link fence, tied the belt securely to the fence's top, pushed himself off, broken his neck, and died. Running across the street, the old friend identified the dead body, now hanging by the leather belt, as Trent Lehman, former child star.

About a week later, Trent Lehman's mother, Bobbi, considering the possibility of some symbolic significance to her son's selection of his elementary school as his suicide site, concluded, "He didn't have that sense of drama." I will not question the mother's judgment, but in Bobbi's own words, "There *was* a lot of rejection. After the *Nanny* show closed, several times producers told us he had gotten one part or another; then they went and hired someone else. It was hard to be so popular, and then so unwanted. He would cry and say, 'What's the matter with me?' It broke my heart, but I encouraged him to keep trying. I didn't want him to feel that he was ending in the business as a failure. I just wanted him to stay in until he could say, 'Hey, I'm not just Butch.' I thought, 'If he just goes out on a few more interviews, he'll click again; then he can drop it.' " Only one minor role came his way afterwards. Once Hollywood dropped Trent, it refused to pick him up again; and when the series folded up, he folded inside.

Bobbi, a former Hollywood children's agent, had begun to worry that Trent had an inherent ambivalence about show-business that even the *Nanny* hit had not cured. He refused to study dancing and singing. He hated going to interviews. At the age of thirteen, Trent announced to his mother that he wanted out of acting. A natural athlete, he had decided to throw himself into sports. But at this point in his life, his sense of timing was completely off. "At thirteen, he was too old for the Little League," said his mother, "but too small for the bigger leagues. He weighed only 110 pounds that first year. Suddenly, he was forced to sit on a bench and was unable to compete. The next year his body grew, he played a lot and he was excellent. But the rejection of that first year—acting, and baseball, was too much at once. It changed his personality. He withdrew. He got sullen, lost his spark. Before, he had been a totally normal boy who walked into producers' offices and got jobs."

Perhaps, but any red-blooded Little Leaguer might have been repelled by Hollywood at times. Before winning the *Nanny* part, Trent was cast as the young George Jorgensen in the 1970 movie *The Christine Jorgensen Story*. They outfitted him in a long white dress, lipstick and feminine make-up. When Trent suddenly made a point of showing everyone on the set the tennis shoes he wore underneath the dress, one of the other little boys in the movie, who played a neighborhood bully, blurted out, "You're a boy!" Until then, none of the other boys had known.

Around 1977, his mother became anxious about the effect of the Hollywood off-stage scene on her children, particularly Trent, the second oldest among her three boys and two girls. When Bobbi discovered that he was consorting with teenagers whom she believed were heavy users of dope and liquor, she ordered clean air and a new life. Her children offered surprisingly little dissent when she proposed that they pick up stakes and resettle in Colorado.

At the start, things seemed a bit better, particularly when Trent joined the Job Corps in Colorado Springs. Still, he seemed lost, unable to decide what new training or direction he wanted. Four years passed. At the start of the summer of 1981, then in his late teens, he moved back to Hollywood. "His friends were like a magnet pulling him back," said his mother, "But when he came back to Colorado for a visit later that summer, he was terrible. Everyone said he wasn't the same person. He told me he was having a nervous breakdown. I got him to tell me he was into drugs—grass, cocaine. . . . I made him go to an M.D. who works with alcoholics. The M.D. insisted that he enter therapy, but he wouldn't. He was always hiding from reality. He was a clown who covered his emotions."

He had certainly concealed them well enough from his mother. Despite all the years of driving Trent to interviews and sitting on sets, she did not fully realize the extent to which Hollywood had undermined his sense of self until after the suicide. "When I went to his apartment after he died, I realized no one could live like that and be sane," she says. "There was no food, only beer. That apartment was a clear demonstration of someone saying, 'I have no self-esteem.' "

She has regrets now, of course. "I made the biggest mistake by not letting him get out when he first wanted to . . . I thought I was doing the best thing. I blame myself, more than the industry. He got taller, had skin breakouts, his voice changed. He was too old to be a kid, too young to be a teenager. He just didn't fit in."

Few of us glide through adolescence with any grace. But for the Hollywood child, that roller coaster ride is particularly bumpy. "Sometimes I can't figure out what to do with a kid who didn't grow up the way we wanted him or her to grow up," says TV producer Al Burton. "There are children whom I see five years after they were absolutely adorable thirteen year olds and, unfortunately, it didn't go too well for them. Then there's someone like Valerie Bertinelli, who grew up just sensationally beautifully, right in front of America."

Valerie Bertinelli is indeed an exception, in more ways than one. Rather than letting her fade out as she turned into her teenage years, Hollywood turned on the spotlight. The executives of the TV series *One Day at a Time* (1975–) were willing to hire what industry insiders call a "true-to-age" teenager to play the part of Barbara Cooper, when the usual practice is to use someone eighteen or over. The latter course is cheaper and easier; California child labor regulations pose a number of restrictions so cumbersome that most production companies prefer to circumvent them by hiring young-looking adults. But, says Al Burton, "I personally have always felt that it is important to reflect reality. So we were willing to give Valerie that base, that unique—and necessary—opportunity of working every single week." If more producers matched Burton's integrity and far-sightedness, the fade-out disease that attacks Hollywood actors in their teens would be considerably arrested.

It is the rare child actor whose career marches steadily forward. "You always hope a kid will catch on," says Hollywood agent Toni Kelman. "If you get in a series that will carry you on up and you have a name, then you will probably keep working. But very few go up the ranks that way and stay in the business. Some don't grow tall enough, or they become very ethnic looking. Some develop heavy acne, or grow to be six feet at age fourteen, and you can't sell them." Few get better parts with age. "A kid of six does a lot, but a kid of eight does less, because he's bigger," says agent Don Schwartz, who represented Trent Lehman in his acting prime. "They just like them better at six. The roughest time in the world is for the elevens."

Agents need not be greatly concerned, perhaps; they are not going to run out of new faces to market. If the unusually conscientious agent considers it his duty to forewarn parents that their children's careers are strictly short-term investments, such advice will likely be ignored, no matter how forcibly offered. "Mothers tend to think only of the excitement of seeing their children in Hollywood," explains agent Althea Shaw. It is indeed an exceptional mother who will permit her beautiful dream to be brought down to earth by long-range considerations or intuitive forebodings. Almost every mother just knows that her child will be one of the few to "catch on," a delusion undeterred by agents who know, of course, the real odds: only one child actor in perhaps 20,000 will continue to succeed. The net result is 19,999 potential failures, broken children and sometimes even broken homes, not to mention the occasional suicides.

When I was ten, I was almost over the hill for a child actress. This realization came to me during my second appearance on an episode of the hit series *Combat!* (1962–1967). I had a good part, and we were rehearsing a key scene. I was cast as a disoriented French waif who has miraculously managed to elude an otherwise devastating barrage of artillery shelling that has all but wiped out my village. From amidst a cloudburst of dense gunsmoke, the late Vic Morrow, in the starring role of Sergeant Chip Saunders, looms on the horizon, carrying a bit of a burden on one shoulder—forty-five pounds of Andrea Darvi, child actress.

He had to carry me upright across a field littered with the bodies of dead G.I.s. I felt ridiculous; like any normal child, I hadn't been carried since I was four. But the producers of the show sought to dramatize my waif-like helplessness in the hands of a brawny, big-hearted American G.I. Unpatriotic or not, I hated the scene, and I knew Vic Morrow felt no love for having to rehearse and rehearse the moment when he had to lift me. He would always wait until just before director Richard Donner yelled, "Action!" Morrow would then heave me off the ground, grunting every inch of the way. With my feet dangling dangerously low, I had to be careful not to kick the extras, who were doing their level best not to burst out laughing and stay true to their roles as dead G.I.s strewn over the set. The tension, and absurdity, soon got to everyone, and when Donner saw that Morrow was struggling terribly to maintain his balance and the dead G.I.s to maintain their composure, he rewrote the script on the spot. "Honey, this isn't going to work anymore," he said to me. Then, to Morrow, "Let her walk it." I was glad to be on my feet, Vic was glad to be forty-five pounds lighter, and the "dead" G.I.s were off the hook.

I was only *almost* over the hill then; three years later, when I turned thirteen, I was on the other side. The *Combat!* show, which was still churning out episodes that required tiny foreign waifs, telephoned my agent one day about Andrea Darvi's availability. When they asked my agent to put a "hold" on me, meaning that if I got another offer, the *Combat!* executives wanted the right of first refusal, I was both flabbergasted and puzzled. Why wasn't I hired outright? Hadn't my track record conferred any advantages?

I waited days for the verdict. When I came home from school one day, my agent delivered it. "They're afraid she's too big," she told my mother over the telephone as Andrea Darvi, at four feet, six inches, weighing sixty pounds, listened in on an extension. "They're afraid she's too big to arouse the same depth of sympathy anymore." I had perpetrated the most heinous crime for any child actor; I had grown.

Acting children are not born Peter Pans. It is the calculating magic of Hollywood that manufactures them. If a drug that arrested growth were available, Hollywood executives might consider slipping it into their stars' Kool-Aid. "They would like you to play Peter Pan as long as that's physically viable," says one children's manager, "and then you're out with the garbage." Al Burton remembers one lovely twelve-year-old girl he interviewed. On her résumé was the accurate boast of 668 performances in a road production of *Annie.* "She had been so concerned about getting too big for the part," Burton remembers her saying, "that when she was told she had outgrown it and the job was at an end, she actually seemed to spurt up four inches. She believed she must have been mentally keeping herself short."

It is an industry you most certainly do not want to grow

up in. Broadway *Annie* director and lyricist Martin Charnin, several months before the show closed on Broadway, explained "You can only lower the hem so far. After four foot six, they're gone." Charnin even refused to audition anyone over that height. "If the child lasts eighteen months on stage, that's pushing it," he said. "These kids know it's not a lifetime job."

Whether in Hollywood or on Broadway, growing up, or out, is a kind of disease that eats into earnings. "I *wanted* to have a chest," remembers Linda Blair. "I didn't want to wear the things that made me look flat. I wanted to be older, but they would say, 'No, Linda, you can't be.' " There is not much you can do. Prematurely busty girls may find their careers prematurely sagging. "We tell them to wear loose clothing," says Hollywood agent Evelyn Schultz of Wormser, Heldfond & Joseph. "They'll call us and specify, 'We want someone fourteen, looking young, no boobs.' " Remembers Darlene Gillespie, "The worst thing that could happen to a female Mouseketeer was to develop a figure."

For the child actor involved in a TV series, the problems are heightened. "I went from four feet, three inches to four feet, eight inches and they had to change my wardrobe three times," says former child actress Gina MacDonald (Darlene's sister), who, at the age of thirteen, was cast as the younger sister in the TV series *Karen* (1964–1965), NBC's short-lived rival to the hit *Gidget* show starring Sally Field. "I had to keep my hair long, but I wanted so much to be a teenager. I once went to a *Karen* rehearsal with my hair up. Irving Paley, the producer, looked at me and said, 'What are you doing?' I protested, 'It's just a rehearsal.' Paley shot back, 'I don't pay you to look thirteen. I pay you to look eleven.' "

The object of the game is to string the public along for as much time as possible—just one more episode of the series, one more segment of arrested personal growth. "The second season they had to get rid of my overalls and give me jeans and a tee shirt to wear instead because I grew so tall they couldn't get overalls to fit right anymore," recalls Jay North about his title role in *Dennis the Menace*. The child is usually the last to learn that growing up means over and out. When it became clear to the producers of *Dennis the Menace* that their star, at eleven years of age, was not a convincing figure as Dennis anymore, they launched a clandestine search for a replacement. But when they failed to find anyone quite right, they folded the series, in 1963. "It was kept from me that they were testing other kids," says an embittered North. "My mother, and all the adults knew. I only found out a few years ago, when Herb Anderson, the man who played my father on the show, who is still a friend, told me, in casual conversation."

Like many child actors, at the age of thirteen I was ironically as near the peak of my career as I was on my way down. With an impressive list of credits, I had managed to land with Paul Kohner, Inc., the prestigious Sunset Strip firm whose clients included stars like Liv Ullman and George Segal. I was as excited as a baby to have so prominent an agent behind me. Alas, this break could not have come at a less opportune time; I was becoming a woman, with budding breasts and other signs of healthy human growth. But the Hollywood symptoms were clear, and fatal: my agent ceased calling; other mothers, no longer taking my career seriously, stopped baiting my mother; I even went on what is politely termed "honorary withdrawal" (exempt from paying dues) from the Screen Actors Guild. Suddenly I was *watching* TV, and I soon noticed that none of the little kids were me, except on the reruns.

The growing pains were duly recorded. At the age of fifteen, I wrote in my diary on March 27, 1967, about a fit of nostalgia that overcame me while combing my mother's big metal files for all my old acting photos. "I have reached an in-between stage—too old for a child, too young for an adult. Acting was my outlet, my distinctiveness from others, my joy and emotional expressiveness. Now I'm just like everybody else, and I can't bear it. I'm dying! If I got a part, I'd pour my whole heart and soul into it. I would love a great acting part now more than anything in the world."

Between the ages of fifteen and seventeen, I sank into a

severe depression. Despite good health, good looks (or so people said), brains and quite a promising future, I was miserable. While at campuses across the country students not much older than I engaged in serious, even heroic efforts to protest the Vietnam War, I was sulking in my little blue bedroom and reading existentialists like Sartre and Camus, including his essay on suicide, and writing "poetry" so bad that by comparison the average *Combat!* script probably read like T. S. Eliot. Occasionally, I broke out of my isolation and joined the world. I took part in mass demonstrations like the great 1967 anti-war rally in San Francisco. (In retrospect, I wonder, was I subconsciously linking a government that could have staged the Vietnam war to an American industry, Hollywood, that had ultimately unstaged me?) A measure of political activism, however, was no consolation; a few nights a week, I was crying myself to sleep. I'd always been good with tears, but now, no one was around to appreciate them. Assuming that my unhappiness was a normal, inevitable part of growing up, I repressed the thought that I might be grieving the loss of my career, and therefore the only measure of self-worth I had ever known.

My imagination found sorrow where others might only see survival. I had been collecting unemployment insurance at the State of California Department of Employment until, after the mandatory monthly review of the claim, a functionary in the Van Nuys office terminated it. I was then fourteen. "She hasn't worked for some length of time and we don't expect her to work," the clerk said, perhaps understandably unsympathetic to see so many pudgy-faced kids standing in line for handouts alongside laid-off blue collar workers whose very existence depended on them. The clerk scolded my mother, "The calls are very few and far between for her age." The clerk was right, and I knew it, but hearing the truth from a stranger made it more real than ever.

My mother filed an appeal with the California Unemployment Insurance Appeals Board, and a hearing was scheduled. I felt awkward at the proceeding, as if I should lie down on the conference table so they could examine my body for signs of temporary decay. My mother launched into a summation worthy of F. Lee Bailey; it was the Scopes trial and *Brown vs. the Board of Education* rolled into one. Eyes flashing and metaphors bouncing, she condemned the state unemployment officials for not knowing how prestigious an agent Paul Kohner was and what an honor it was to be accepted as a client. Why would they take on someone unemployable, she asked rhetorically? She then rattled off some impressive names on Kohner's client list and reminded them that it had been a poor TV season for everybody. She described, accurately, the nature of the business; you could be down one season, on top the next. How dare they predict what experts in the field could not? When she finished her peroration, I had to wonder who was the better actress in the family.

A month later, a letter from the Appeals Board arrived, reinstating my claim. My mother had triumphed, but *I* felt defeated. I was now an unemployed actress, officially. In subsequent years, only a few calls came my way, and only one minor part. This, for me, was a bleak twilight zone that only a Rod Serling could have imagined.

In a small, dark, modest one-bedroom apartment overlooking downtown Los Angeles, one of Hollywood's most talented and successful former child actors is composing his thoughts for a book about what he calls the self-management of recreational drugs, drawing on his own serious brushes with drug abuse and the law as an adult.

His name is Tom (Tommy) Rettig. At five, he was cast in the Joshua Logan road show of *Annie Get Your Gun*, starring Mary Martin. He appeared in movies like *River of No Return* (1954), directed by Otto Preminger and starring Marilyn Monroe. He is perhaps best remembered for his portrayal of Jeff Miller in the first leg (1954–1957) of the long-running *Lassie* television series.

"As far as Tom Rettig, the person, is concerned, I never understood what my child acting years were all about," he told me. "My life had never made sense to me. I was told when I was a kid, 'If you want the part, you've got to tell the producer you can and want to do this, in order to have it,' but knowing that somewhere I had reservations. I don't know any eight year old who does know what he wants to do for the rest of his life.

"I always thought my work was temporary. I was only under contract to *Lassie*. After about two or three years of the show, I wanted out, but I didn't say anything. My mother advised me that it wouldn't be in my best interest to say that. Two thousand dollars a week was certainly something to be considered.

"But I was fourteen. I wanted to go to parties on Friday nights, and I couldn't, because there was always filming that started early Saturday morning. I wanted to play during the summer, but didn't get to because we always filmed all through the summer. I felt that I was able to have my childhood with me while I was working, but I couldn't have my adolescence with me because that meant things like sexuality and dating. Those were not things I could have with me and still be Jeff Miller."

In his third year on the series, Rettig, along with some of the adult series regulars, sued in court for releases from their contracts, and won. "At this point, my mother was listening to me," Rettig says. "When *Lassie* was over I turned down a three-picture deal in Europe. I went to high school and put my career on hold."

For a while, the change was exhilarating. He was just one of the boys, smoking cigarettes, even drinking to excess on occasion, despite everything he'd been told by adults. But the high soon ended. "When I was eighteen and out of school and married," he says, "for nine months I worked in a variety of jobs. I was selling clothes, working in a hardware store, delivering flowers. Then I was even a disc jockey for a while. But after awhile, it looked like the most sensible thing to do was get work as an actor, fast. Even if I was cut back to five hundred a week, it would beat the ninety a week I was getting delivering flowers."

The decision to quit acting, he realized, had been made in a vacuum. Just as outsiders tended to glamourize Hollywood, Rettig had idealized conditions in the "real" world, which he believed compared incredibly favorably, to those in the make-believe world he knew so well. But like many child actors, he had been shielded, having never labored in fast food joints or discount shoe stores. While he was pulling in thousands of dollars a week, he had no idea that others had to work just as hard for a tenth as much money.

He also failed to consider in advance how hard it would be to get back into acting once he had left. "I was hearing a lot of 'No's,' " he told me of his attempted comeback in his early twenties. "I was doing two or three shows a year and making five or six thousand a year. I didn't have a lot of self-esteem. I'm not six feet tall, I'm not your typical leading man. I look thirty and talk forty. Where do I fit in?"

Hollywood had no suggestions for Lassie's best friend. "I took it personally," Rettig says, "when in fact they would have rejected anyone who had been Jeff Miller for several years. The biggest negative is adjusting to things when they change. It can be tragic in your teens, which is when it typically occurs for child actors. When I was twenty-five, I went through a re-evaluation of my life. I had children and a wife. I wasn't particularly happy with my limited abilities to work at what I liked to do. So I went to my agent and manager and publicity person and said, 'Take me off your lists.' I wanted to be able to seek work that would allow me to have the kind of self-esteem I was used to having as a child."

But his childhood fame had become a roadblock to adult success. "I still feel it was a wise decision, not only for my psychological welfare, but so that, if I ever want to return to acting, they won't say, 'We saw Tommy last year.' Instead they would say, 'We haven't seen him in ten years, what does he look like now?' The doors would be a little more open. I *wouldn't* be a familiar face." In a business where millions of unknowns are looking for stardom, Rettig is a former star wanting to become an unknown.

And he is not giving up. "When I first quit, I said to myself, 'It might be ten years, twenty years, until I'm sixty and have gray hair and wrinkles and can do some good character parts,' " Rettig remembers thinking. "I've never really given up the idea of acting." It is an ambition not easily surrendered.

"There is the almost universal experience that acting is an addiction," says Los Angeles-based clinical psychologist and specialist in the entertainment field Thomas Backer. "And it is made greater if the child actor made the decision to leave against his will, because he couldn't get work."

At first, Jay North welcomed the end of the *Dennis the Menace* series. "I wanted to get out of the isolated world of the soundstage and into the real world," he told me. "There were times when I wanted to get through a math problem instead of filming. There were a lot of times I wanted to be left alone. I was conscious of it even then, but there was no way I could talk about the pressure. My family tried to keep my life as normal as possible off the set, but it was impossible—everywhere I went people wanted pictures, autographs. On weekends, I'd go across the country on junkets, doing telethons. Sometimes I didn't want anyone to recognize me."

From ages seven to eleven, North had lived like the boy in the plastic bubble, locked into the soundstage, uncontaminated by exposure to other children. "Private school was my first exposure to other kids outside of the business, and to life," he remembers. "We were on different wavelengths. In acting, you mature faster. I found nothing in common with people my age. I preferred adults. So I started to feel it was better to work." But like so many former television child stars, he was typecast out of the market. He was as historically memorable, and untouchable, as a museum antique.

A series sometimes has no end; that is when the trouble can begin. "I've turned down television series offers for my clients, to agents' horror," says Hollywood children's manager Michael Harrah, "because I saw the series was going to be successful and I knew what it would do to the child. Success can be crippling if you don't choose it properly."

North could have used that sage advice. "Six months after *Dennis*," he says, "I tested for *The Sound of Music*, when I was about twelve. Robert Wise [the director] looked at the film but said the *Dennis* image was so strong he couldn't use me. I was called back six times."

We then had to laugh over what was a tremendous coincidence. As it happened, I also had been called back for *The Sound of Music* six times. The same day as North's screentest, I was doing my homework in the children's trailer that Jay was also using on the Twentieth Century Fox lot, having been called back one more time for the part of nine-year-old Brigitta in the Von Trapp family. It was the final cut; Angela Cartwright and I were the only two left. During the screentest, Angela did well, but at eleven years old with five years in the business, I, too, was capable of some real acting. I aced the final test. Everything was right, except my looks. Angela looked like she might have come from Austria; wherever my looks came from, it wasn't Austria. "*She just doesn't look Austrian*," director Wise had to tell my agent, giving the Brigitta role to Angela. Afterwards, yes, I cried. Wouldn't you? Several months later, I wrote in my diary, "I turned the record player on and heard *The Sound of Music*. It still makes me feel sad. As Mommy said, I can't go on never listening to it again."

Sour grapes? Or the justifiable grapes of wrath? Perhaps both, but I found North nodding vigorously at my familiar story. "When I was fourteen or fifteen," he says, "I went to an interview at United Artists and chatted with the producer. I was really looking forward to getting a chance to read for this part. The producer said, 'You aren't right for the part, but I'm just curious—who would you recommend?' I was totally crushed. Today, I have this fantasy. I'm playing ice hockey, and a casting director or director or producer is out there on the ice. And I'm hitting him with my stick."

Now in his early thirties, Jay North is financially comfortable from his *Dennis the Menace* investments, but he still wonders about his next part. "I enjoy acting," he says. "And I haven't found any other professional fulfillment."

"I was twenty-four when I decided to do something with myself," says ex-Mouseketeer Darlene Gillespie. For the six years after *The Mickey Mouse Club* (1955–1959) folded, Darlene had managed no more than a smattering of uninspiring jobs—a few forgettable TV appearances, a singing and dancing part in a Vegas act featuring Johnny Desmond. Eventually she decided she didn't like the business anymore. Or, as a long-time friend and fellow Mouseketeer sympathetically put it, "The break she needed wasn't there for her."

Darlene, as if attempting to make light of her own wounds by tending to others', then entered the nursing profession. But Operation Starting Over was not a success. She found herself just as typecast there as she had been in Hollywood. "The other nurses used to call me the Mickey Mouse nurse," she recalls. "People would always say, 'Why aren't you a big star like Annette?' Even doctors would ask that. I'd want to say, 'Why aren't you the administrator of this hospital?' Well, I spent my life apologizing for not being Annette. For a long time, it was hard to feel any self-worth; I started to lose belief in my intelligence. I was an unsuccessful Mouseketeer, because I wasn't Annette. Ultimately, the experience was ego-crushing, more bad than good."

Then the past returned anew to haunt her. When *The Mickey Mouse Club* series was rerun on TV several years ago, Darlene's four-year-old daughter, completely unprompted by Mom, started to tune in. Like many other kids, now as then, her daughter loved the show. Darlene hated even the thought of it, to the extent of trying to bury her past. "I never told her it was me she was seeing on TV," Darlene says, "because I was terrified she wouldn't like me. Maybe she'd think I was stupid. After all, she was used to *Sesame Street*." Rather than forbid her daughter to watch the reruns, a rule that would have seemed arbitrary and senseless, Darlene gambled that her child would never guess the real identity of Mouseketeer "Darlene." She lost her gamble, inadvertently betrayed by a neighbor who bluntly asked the child, "Don't you know that's your mother?" Says Darlene, "After that, my own daughter was introducing me to people as the Mouseketeer Darlene. I told her it embarrassed me."

Unlike Jay North and Tommy Rettig, I never had the luck, or misfortune, of securing a series. If I had, I might have given up on Hollywood sooner. I didn't; my dream died harder. When I was fifteen and hadn't worked for two years, I wrote in my diary, "Lately, I've been imagining situations that deal with performing. I sing and pretend there's an audience and that I'm giving a performance. Or I make up lines and do a dramatic scene, but I don't let anyone see. Someday I do, deep down, believe I'll have that chance to act again. Meanwhile, I'll just have to live without it, which is hard."

Then one day my agent Walter Kohner (Paul Kohner's brother) telephoned with the news that the producers of a Dick Van Dyke special were looking for kids who could sing in French with Michel Legrand at the piano. I had been studying opera privately, and studying French in school. The job sounded perfect for me, Kohner said, so he booked me into the audition.

A lot of kids who showed up to interview turned out to be colleagues of mine whom I had known for ages, . . . since I was six. I was both startled and comforted by the fact that they, too, had grown up, and in a few individual instances out. I wasn't the only one afflicted, it seemed, by the disease of adolescence.

The requirements of the audition were simple—to sing half the alphabet to the scale being knocked out on the piano. As if an erstwhile Renata Tebaldi, I regarded the audition as my chance to star in *Tosca*. But as I launched confidently into a few start-up notes, the piano player stopped in mid-scale and someone in the back of the room growled out, "Cut the soprano stuff!" No vibrato, please. Just sing it plain and simple, like a kid. Well, jobs were scarce, so I folded my Renata Tebaldi imitation and trotted out my former self—the preteen, slightly nasal-toned Andrea—to take up the challenge. I got the part. I cut the soprano stuff. I was back in the business. As the diary entry on February 24, 1967 put it, "I was picked! It's a nothing part, but it feels good and gives me encouragement for the long ahead future."

In a state near euphoria, my mother and I decided to make an unscheduled visit to the Kohner Agency. We were always looking for excuses to get Walter excited about me again. Besides, I wanted to have the pleasure of delivering a personal report on my triumph to witness his pleased reaction myself.

Walter greeted me with his usual charm and warmth, and we talked for a few minutes about what I had been doing the past two years. Then I popped the big news about the Dick Van Dyke show. I wanted him to think of me as a once washed-up grand diva on her second reincarnation, better wine in the same bottle. Instead of enthusiasm, however, the reaction I got was lack of interest. In a soft, sweet, paternalistic tone of voice, he said, "That's wonderful, wonderful. . . . And you can keep the money without giving us our commission."

In other words, keep the pennies, kid. Not for the first time, alas, my mother misinterpreted my mood. "That was awfully nice of him!" she exclaimed. If only she could have understood my feelings, that *I* would have paid *him* to take his commission, simply to restore my sense of self-worth. Years later, I realized Walter Kohner had meant well. Seeing how happy I was to have a part, *any* part, he also saw that *The Dick Van Dyke Special* would be one of my last roles. He didn't have the heart to rake up the spare change that symbolized what little was left of my career.

Though the special went well, I was nearing the end of the road. When I was sixteen, I was sent out by Kohner to Universal Studios for what turned out to be one of my very last interviews. I had worked for this casting director many times, and I knew he had always liked me. During interviews, he would often bless me with a special smile and cute wink that I used to imagine none of the other kids got. The feeling was reciprocal.

For this particular movie, he was looking to cast a convent girl. I was more the type of actress who might lure all the nuns out of the convent than into one, but if any casting director would hire me as a budding nun, he was the one.

When I got to Universal, the expression on his face registered astonishment over how much I had grown in the past few years alone. We chatted for a few minutes about school, and how I found "retirement." It was a warm and friendly conversation, but then came the fatal question, "How old are you?"

When I told him I was sixteen, he rolled his eyes up to the ceiling, smiled sarcastically and said, "Now come on, Andrea, you can tell me your real age."

"Sixteen," I replied, not comprehending.

"Now Andrea," he said, "you've been around for a long time!"

Indeed, sir, I have; a card-carrying actress in Hollywood since the age of six!

Having forgotten how young I was when I started, he now viewed me as the typical prevaricating child actress. Nothing I said could convince him of my real age, even when I offered the documentation of my driver's license.

I really *was* sixteen—not sweet sixteen, but washed-up sixteen.

Few careers can measure up to acting for the money, glamour, fame and ego gratification. "A career like that at an early age tends to paralyze you in seeking out other alternatives, because they don't seem so attractive, rewarding or aggrandizing," says former thirties child star Dick (Dickie) Moore.

Parental approval (in some cases, parental fawning), also discourages the child from bidding adieu to Hollywood. "There comes a time when you realize it's not exactly what you want, but you can't communicate that feeling to your parents," says former sixties child actor Gary Marsh. "You can see their expectations even in the smallest of statements, like when they would say, 'Wouldn't it be neat if you got the part?' You keep doing it because of the money—and because they're proud of you."

At twenty-one, Marsh finally gave up. His was a hilarious exit. "A casting director said to me, 'I know you want to get out of acting, but I've got the perfect part for you,' " Marsh remembers. " 'It will take only two days!' I told him I didn't want to work two days for scale. But this casting director said, 'We'll pay you scale for two weeks—but you'll only work two days.' I showed up the first day and said, 'Okay, wardrobe people, what do I wear?' Everyone started laughing. Then someone said, 'You mean, nobody told you?' The role was: I'm sitting naked in a jacuzzi between two naked female twins, passing a joint, and then I ask the star if he wants a hit. Well, that was my retirement scene. A very fitting ending. I literally left the business with nothing."

Gary, now operating a successful Los Angeles-based script analysis service for agents, is still well-connected to casting directors around town and is occasionally offered other "perfect" parts. He always declines, telling them, "I don't think it would be good for my mental health." With or without clothes, the thought of acting gives him a chill.

Getting into Hollywood as a child can be easier than getting out years later. "People tend to think they have to go cold turkey," says Dr. Thomas Backer. Once made, the decision is more like a religious vow than a simple career choice. "Generally, there's a tying-off of the experience of having been a child actor," he says. "It becomes a separate part of history."

Kevin Corcoran was one who quit and was glad he did. His withdrawal—gradual, not cold turkey—was almost clinical in its realization. Today, he can say, "Watching a rerun is like watching a character doing a part. You're convinced it's not you."

For eight years, Kevin Corcoran, perhaps best remembered as "Moochie" in *The Mickey Mouse Club* TV series *Adventures in Dairyland* (1956), was a prized Disney Studios contract player.

He did major roles in such classic children's films of the sixties as *Toby Tyler* (1960), *Pollyanna* (1960), and *Swiss Family Robinson* (1960). "I was born into it," says Corcoran, who began doing commercials at age two. "The whole family was in it. It was the way we made our living."

Kevin's father, head of maintenance at MGM during the fifties, was eager to secure good lives for his eight children. He succeeded. Kevin's sister Noreen Corcoran was the costar of the long-running television series *Bachelor Father* (1957–1962). Another Corcoran son was also under contract to Disney. All the Corcoran children were highly successful child actors. "Our parents were proud of us," says Kevin. "We did good work, and our name meant something."

Kevin Corcoran had been fortunate enough to work consistently throughout his teens, but when he turned eighteen and finally came to understand that he simply did not care for acting any longer, he got out. "It was dehumanizing to be interviewed by casting directors," he told me. "I don't like to be put on a block for sale, and by people who don't know what they're doing. Some actors have a need that overrides these negatives. For me, it wasn't worth going through all this crap just in order to do my trade." In fact, Kevin had felt this way for a long time, but could not bring himself to give up the family business, much less relinquish the role of breadwinner; his father had died when Kevin was nine.

While acting had always made Kevin the odd man out at public school, in college he hoped to become one of the boys. Though he took a major in theater arts at California State University at Northridge in southern California, his interest was not in acting but in the production side of the business. "As I got more and more involved in other ends of the industry, people would always say disparagingly, 'Why don't you act?' " he says. "I thought, 'If you want to act, I certainly am not going to let you know what you're in for.' " When he graduated from college in the early seventies, Kevin Corcoran went home. Disney Studios hired him as a "production observer." This is a polite job description for a gofer.

Without knowing it, Disney Studios in effect was providing a kind of methadone maintenance program for an ex-addict, willing to take just about any punishment, except the pain of mainlining again by acting. The program began to work, and his new career started to open up. "At first, I was a nonentity," he says, "but then the Disney people saw that I had natural ability." Within four years, Corcoran became a full-fledged movie and TV producer. The path to success was relatively quick, if not easy. "Everyone at Disney would always say, 'Why are you going into the other end of the business?' " he says sarcastically. "I would have to keep saying, 'Acting is an unpleasant way of life for me.' "

Kevin is philosophically chipper about his past. "I got to travel all over the world," he told me. "I experienced what average kids never do. I'm not insane now. I am doing well now, so maybe being in the business was good after all." Today, he takes pride in his hard-earned sense of perspective. "Lots of times it didn't matter whether actors were talented or untalented. You had so little control over your career, and yet your neck was always on the line. At least now I have some control over my destiny."

Leaving the industry entirely and abruptly may be the more common method of rejecting Hollywood. Many ex-child actors tend to take off virtually as soon as they can manage it. The cold turkey route may not be so torturous for them. "A lot of child actors get going in the business more out of accident," explains Dr. Backer. "They have a parent in the business in some capacity, or they are very attractive, personable, or in the right place at the right time." Defining "accident" as anything other than an early and long-standing genuine interest in the field, Backer suspects that the reason so many readily drop out of Hollywood, usually after they turn eighteen, is that they never actually made the original decision to go into it.

Once free of their parents, who in effect laid that move on them years ago, the son or daughter, no longer a child, can repudiate the decision. Jon Provost, who replaced Tom Rettig in the *Lassie* series as the dog's new owner in 1957, was utterly unremorseful when he left the show in 1964. "He never said a word," remembers his mother Cecile. "They wanted three more years from him, but my husband felt Jon should be in school with other children." At the age of seventeen, after a few more years of making occasional guest appearances on TV specials, Provost announced that he was quitting the business entirely. "Jon had been manipulated by all of us," admits Cecile, "but he was too young to know then. He was trained, almost like Lassie, to do as he was told."

Jon chose the cold turkey route. He told his mother to inform his agent there would be no more calls. Then he moved away, to Sonoma State College in northern California. "He didn't let me go up to enroll with him," says Cecile. "We never went to that college one time. He didn't invite us. I told him if at college he wanted to go on an interview, to call me or Lola [Moore, his agent]. She called him, but he wouldn't come."

I never had the thrill of telephoning my agent with the dramatic declaration, "Take me off your list." My agent simply stopped calling. In his defense, Hollywood was casting Third World waifs who looked eight, not eighteen. But if my farewell was gradual and unspoken, it was every bit as final.

I had been out of circulation for three years when I applied to college, but I was still sorry to leave so much behind. A friend's envying observation haunted me. "Anyone can go to college, but not everyone can act like you."

But did I really want to make the rounds again, toting a book of pictures of Miss Junior Third World in the hope that someone would remember? Did I really want to beg for one- and two-line parts when I had once carried leads? The answer was no, of course. At eighteen, I wanted to start fresh, not start over, and have nothing to do with the business that had forced me to retire at the vulnerable age of fifteen. It was some con- solation, though not much, that I knew my case was not special. However independent many ex-child actors may portray themselves, few leave Hollywood entirely willingly. The business first deserts them. That rejection makes them bitter. Staying away is more an act of self-defense than courage.

The year that I applied to college, the University of California at Santa Cruz was the hot campus in the United States. *Look* magazine had dubbed it "the Oxford of the West." It was supposed to be an intellectual haven, a far cry from Hollywood—which was where I wanted to be. My only problem was, with 10,000 other prospective freshmen applying, I had to find a way to distinguish myself from the pack. Acting, which had always made me feel like an alien, could now be exploited as a way of helping me stand out in a crowd.

On the day I received the school's letter of reply to my application, which had listed my Hollywood credits and contained letters of recommendation from my former producers and directors, I was scheduled to go on one of the last auditions of my life, a callback for the movie version of the musical *Fiddler on the Roof*. Shortly before preparing to leave for the interview, one of my best friends, who also had applied for admission to U.C.–Santa Cruz, called to announce that she had received her acceptance letter. I had not received one, so after I congratulated her and hung up, I naturally became despondent and self-critical. When the postman arrived with the mail, my mother beat me in the race to the front door, padded into another room and locked the door. When I heard what sounded like the rustling of paper, I shouted angrily, "What are you doing?" She burst through the door, screaming happily, "This is a letter of acceptance!" We threw our arms around one another, the first time in years we had embraced like that, probably the first time since an agent had called to tell me I had gotten a job. My fade-out period was over. I was now a college student who happened to be an ex-child actress.

Still, I kept the audition appointment and was never in a better mood to perform. When it came my turn to sing, director Norman Jewison actually applauded, even though it must have been about the hundredth rendition of "Matchmaker, Matchmaker" he'd heard that afternoon. Despire the super audition,

I estimated that my chances for getting that movie part, which likely would be cast in Europe, were remote. I simply felt it would not happen.

As my mother Evelyn, who had accompanied me to the audition, drove home, I remembered to ask her, "Why didn't you hand me the letter from the school as soon as it arrived in the mail, and let *me* open it?" She thought for a moment, then replied, "I was worried that it was a rejection. I figured there was no point in going to the interview in a foul mood."

There it was—five years after the peak of my career, the interviews were still everything. Nothing must stand between me and a job.

"They said you're not Jewish enough looking," said Walter Kohner, later explaining why Jewison had rejected me for the role. "Too Armenian."

"But I *am* Jewish!" I screamed, taking a few minutes to calm myself. Even at age seventeen, I cannot win—not Austrian enough for *The Sound of Music*, not Jewish enough for *Fiddler on the Roof*. This, I decided, was The End! Fade out! Curtain!

Every generation of child actors has its notable survivors. Patty Duke Astin was on the brink of her teens when she was cast as Helen Keller in the 1959 Broadway play *The Miracle Worker*. Since then she has performed in a variety of movies (*The Miracle Worker*, 1962; *Valley of the Dolls*, 1967) and television series (*The Patty Duke Show*, 1963–1966 and *It Takes Two*, 1982–). Ron Howard grew up on *The Andy Griffith Show* from 1960–1968, and six years later became the star of the hit ABC series *Happy Days* (1974–). Today, he is a successful TV and movie producer/director (*Night Shift*, 1982). Kristy McNichol was already eleven when she first caught on as Buddy in the ABC-TV series *Family* (1976–1979). "Year by year, as *Family* went on, they had me gradually grow up," she remembers. "But it was like they didn't really want me to." When the series folded, she was sixteen—and caught in the middle of the awkward period. Since then, she has landed a succession of good movie roles, but even now she counts her blessings, almost incredulous at being able to avoid oblivion. *"Family* led to *Little Darlings* [1980], she said. "After that, everyone just kept calling. Keeping it going is very important to me now, but when I was younger, I didn't worry about whether I would be able to."

Elizabeth Taylor's career began at the age of eight, when the British-born child actress signed a contract with Universal Studios. Although the studio put her on a training program— a crash course in singing, in particular—her expectations were soon disappointed. During her first year under contract, she was not given a single movie role. Discouraged, Taylor soon parted company with Universal. Then, in a major turnaround, MGM producer Sam Marx cast her opposite child star Roddy McDowall in the 1943 movie *Lassie Come Home.* She was eleven. After that, still under contract to MGM, other film roles came along. She appeared opposite McDowall once again in *The White Cliffs of Dover* (1944). Then, she was loaned out to Twentieth-Century Fox to appear in the movie *Jane Eyre.* And finally, around the age of thirteen—what is ordinarily the most awkward period for the majority of Hollywood children—she appeared in the leading role that made her a star, *National Velvet* (1945).

Peggy Ann Garner, another child star of the forties, not only survived the curse of losing her childhood but skillfully managed to exploit her maturation. "When most child actors disappear was my most creative period as a child," she says. "I think society was tired of curls and pretty little children. I was homely."

At twelve, Peggy Ann landed her most famous role, that of Francie Nolan in the movie *A Tree Grows in Brooklyn* (1945). In her late teens, she began to do Broadway plays. Since then, she has worked only sporadically—though invariably with distinction. In 1962, for example, Peggy Ann and I played opposite one another on a segment of *The Untouchables.* The episode, a pilot that presaged the *Charlie's Angels* genre, had Barbara Stanwyck starring as a lady detective. It was private eye Stanwyck's strategy to use me to help her locate a night-club singer for questioning. I was a poor Italian girl who had befriended the nightclub singer (Peggy Ann). Like Peggy Ann, Stanwyck treated a child actor with respect and intelligence, the kind some established stars reserve for adults. She discussed my role with me, and listened attentively when I told her how I thought the character should feel about, and respond to, the detective's queries. Like Barbara, Peggy Ann seemed to delight in my lack of reverence. "Who's Peggy Ann Garner?" she heard me ask someone on the set—one of many who was in awe of this former child legend.

As she would be the first to agree, Garner's later successes never measured up to her early triumphs. What is remarkable is that she kept plugging along. "When I walk on a set today, people say, 'Why aren't you working more?' " says Peggy Ann. "I should be more aggressive. But if you're used to the studio and agent taking care of you, it's hard to pick up a phone and say, 'Hi, here I am.' It shakes me, tears me apart. It's fear of rejection."

From a distance, the bridge connecting child and adult stardom may look sturdy and wide, but on closer inspection it is a tricky crossing no matter how carefully you step. Consider Mickey Rooney, who has always been an awesome talent. In his teens, he starred in films like *Captains Courageous* (1937), *Little Lord Fauntleroy* (1936), and *Ah, Wilderness* (1935). In the late seventies, *Sugar Babies* was a huge Broadway hit. Smooth sailing, right? That is not the way Rooney remembers it. Said he, with considerable bitterness, "Up to *Sugar Babies*, I was a famous has-been. In the sixties and seventies, nobody wanted Mickey Rooney."

Then he fell silent.

I asked, "How did you make your comeback?"

"It was my intuitiveness and sticking-to-it, my God-given ability to keep picking myself up off the canvas." Then he added, "There's no such thing as bridging that gap." He said much the same on the occasion of accepting an honorary Life Achievement Oscar in April of 1983. Explained Rooney: "At nineteen years old I was the number one star for two years. When I was forty, nobody wanted me. I couldn't get a job."

At the pinnacle of success, he nevertheless could not help mentioning his Hollywood mid-life crisis.

After the age of twelve or thirteen, the percentages are against even the most talented child. Says producer Al Burton, remembering a real-life scene some three decades ago, "The rule is, from fourteen to eighteen you get replaced by an eighteen year old who looks fourteen to eighteen."

Burton recalled a telling anecdote about another young talent left in the lurch by The Gap. A very beautiful teenage girl in search of work came to his apartment with her mother. She had a name as a successful child actress, but at this point she was no hotter than any other struggling starlet under eighteen years of age whom Hollywood had put on hold. "She had no career because she was in her teens," says Burton, flatly. "She'd do anything. We were putting together a pilot called *My Daring Daughter*, and hired her. But it never saw the light of day." Leaving aside a one-year run portraying a teenage daughter in the series *Pride of the Family* (1954–1955), she was largely inactive as a teenager. Not until she appeared in the 1955 movie *Rebel Without a Cause*, for which she won an Academy Award nomination and landed a Warner Brothers contract, did Natalie Wood begin to work again. She was then almost eighteen. And this was someone whom *Parents* magazine in 1947 voted "The Most Talented Juvenile Motion Picture Star of the Year" for her role as the cynical little girl who refused to believe in Santa Claus in *Miracle on 34th Street.*

Despite her difficulties, Wood usually sought to maintain that she loved being a child actress and was grateful for the experience. But, in fact, she was somewhat bitter about her past. Even when you succeed professionally, growing up in Hollywood is not easy. "The main trouble working as a child was that I found it very difficult to have a strong sense of my own identity," Wood once said. "I was playing so many parts, I had a hard time finding me." On another occasion, she said, "For a child who works in Hollywood, there is overattention—chaperones and welfare workers—yet at the same time there's an overresponsibility." To Natalie, turning eighteen on the heels of her *Rebel* triumph, leaving The Gap and childhood behind meant more than finding work; it meant escape from prison and the prospect of revenge. As she put it upon approaching her high school graduation, "I'm planning a party and I'll burn an effigy to represent all teachers and welfare workers. They trailed me every place I went. Now at least I can go to work alone."

The Gap, a drawbridge that goes up and does not come back down, has stymied actors of all eras. Even the great Shirley Temple failed to overcome the odds. Having almost single-handedly saved The Fox Film Corporation from the brink of economic ruin during the Depression, Shirley greeted adolescence with one of her most notable bombs *The Blue Bird* (1940). Other unmemorable movie flops then followed in succession. In her early twenties, beaten by The Gap, Shirley Temple retired. "We just couldn't find the stories she needed," her mother Gertrude once told a newspaper reporter. "We felt her career was at a standstill."

Not that her mother hadn't tried almost everything, including lying to her own daughter about her age. Even today, Shirley Temple cannot forget waking up to her twelfth birthday—only to discover it was actually her thirteenth. Gertrude Temple had faithfully observed standard studio practice by lopping one year off of her daughter's age. Only at the brink of Shirley's adolescence did she apprise her of the truth. How did she react to the news? Says Temple, now in her fifties, "I cried a lot because I thought I had lost a whole year."

Temple never regained her preteen success. After a brief fling on television—from 1959–61, she narrated and occasionally starred in the dramatized fairytale series *Shirley Temple's Storybook* (later called *The Shirley Temple Show*)—she retired. Never looking back, she went cold turkey. She said, "I had an enchanted childhood, a magic childhood with great memories. But I don't want to live in the past and I *don't* live in the past." In 1977, when the master of ceremonies at a meeting in California where Shirley was speaking announced that he had received twenty-eight requests from the audience for her to sing just one verse of "The Good Ship Lollipop," she declined the bait with the words, "Nothing could be sadder than a forty-nine-year-old woman singing a child's song; I don't even do that at home." Once, when she was serving as former President Gerald Ford's Chief of Protocol, the ambitious Shirley flashed remorseful, "Sometimes I feel like the oldest living American."

A child star will be dismissed as a dismal failure simply because, in more ways than one, he is not what he once was. Margaret O'Brien was regarded as a flop even though her career continued long after her preteen years. In 1959, reporting on her first marriage at the age of twenty-two, *Time* magazine selected these dismissive words to sum up her situation. "Age made her a Hollywood has-been at thirteen." This was not correct. Although MGM released Margaret from her contract four years after she had won an Academy Award at the age of seven, as she turned into her teenage years she landed good parts in stage shows such as *Child of the Morning, Kiss and Tell, Jenny Kissed Me,* and *The Intruder.* "They weren't awkward years for me, they were awkward years for the *studio*," she reminisced, her bitterness surfacing. Throughout her teens and early twenties, O'Brien continued to do significant stage work, whether *Under the Yum Yum Tree* or *A Thousand Clowns.* She did a lot of television, too, well into her thirties. "I had already built a name, and I did different scripts," she explained to me, recalling some of the guest appearances she made in high-quality TV shows such as *Studio One, Matinee Theater,* and Alfred Hitchcock's series *Suspicion.*

However, it is certainly true that her career is in a holding pattern today. This is a reality that O'Brien understandably has difficulty facing. "I still like to work," she admitted to me not long ago, adding, "But I have enough money that I don't have to work if I don't want to. I love to travel. I don't want to get up at five in the morning all the time."

Even those who manage to bridge the gap between childhood and adulthood have to stretch themselves out immensely. All the advantages of youth are now gone. "A child believes, so he performs easily because he has the facility for play," says one formerly very well-known child actor (who prefers to go unnamed, due to a still stormy relationship with his mother). Now in his fifties, he has just retired. "As an adult, you have a different self-awareness," he told me. "I learned to act again, through trial and error, at work, on television. At least you do it again, but maybe not as well. It's like when you're older and you want to run across the street, but suddenly your feet don't take you that fast anymore. You know how to act in the part, but your instincts alone can't take you there."

In Hollywood, children generally receive heavy-handed instructions from directors, who may request nothing more than that the child mimic the director's way of delivering the lines. They will usually award passing grades to children who give only halfway decent performances. "I don't think a child can really act in the way that Robert DeNiro can act," says Darryl Hickman, now a drama teacher in Los Angeles and an adult actor. "A child relies almost totally on intuition. Basically, what you see on the screen is really the kid."

Can expert guidance for child actors help spring them over the gap into successful adult acting careers? Perhaps. "Proper management involves establishing a unique personality on the basis of a talent that will be viable when the freshness of childhood has worn away," says children's manager Michael Harrah, whose clients include Quinn Cummings, an Oscar nominee for her performance in *The Goodbye Girl* (1977). "You must be shaped and molded and your career must be built." At the age of twelve, Harrah began performing in New York-based musical comedy road shows such as *The King and I* and *Flower Drum Song*. "I was in no way coerced, and it was a wonderful experience; but I was not guided properly," he says. "If you're not, you end up having wasted all that time as a child performer. You must maintain momentum, and keep a constant presence as a performer."

The smart approach, Harrah suggests, is to nurture your young clients even when—indeed, especially when—they are not bringing in the big money. "While the roles may not be there in the teenage years, the mental pre-set must be, so that at the time they turn eighteen they become mentally as well as commercially viable," he says. "You can't, on the child's eighteenth birthday, suddenly shift gears and say, 'All right, you're now allowed to do the things you couldn't as a child, so jump in, kid.' Naturally, a kid's not going to be able to make that transition." The child's growth and sophistication must be emphasized. A sheltered family life is a definite hindrance to a developing child actor, he says, because, "The child won't be ready to deal with the real world."

In his view, one that is shared by most children's managers, Teri Shields is as close to a model mother and manager as exists today. "What she has done is to develop her daughter's potential as an adult, rather than as a child," says Harrah. "Brooke has been intelligently exploited." Overall planning is more important than overnight success. "What's the goal orientation?" asks TV producer Joel Rogosin (*Magnum, P. I., Ironside, Mr. Merlin*). "If it's to have a long-range commercial product, then Brooke Shields' mother is doing okay."

Few teenage actresses will find Brooke Shields easy to emulate. Who can fulfill the child/woman image as comfortably as Brooke? Indeed, imitation in Hollywood is sometimes the most effective form of self-effacement. "The Brooke Shields syndrome has begun to make all of the teenage girls think, 'I'm tall and gorgeous,'" complains one Hollywood agent, who tries to explain to her female teenage clients their mistake when they show up at interviews with enough make-up on their adolescent faces to sink the Love Boat.

The smart Hollywood actress knows better than to try to Brooke the gap. As Quinn Cummings, who knows her own mind, puts it, "I've always been typecast as a smart little girl, short of wearing horn-rimmed glasses." She says she likes being a smart little girl, Jordache rear ends be damned. Admits her manager, Harrah, "We're in a difficult period with Quinn Cummings. Her image is still that of Lucy McFadden in *The Goodbye Girl*. We are begging for interviews for Quinn Cummings. Now, that's a child who has won awards and been nominated for the highest award we have to give! Quinn is very resilient, but there are moments when she says, 'I just want to work.' I say, 'Do you want to go back to doing one-line parts and extra work?' " And Quinn Cummings, like the teenage Natalie Wood of another era, has a name.

The Gap is in part a monstrous creation of well-intentioned California law, which in the effort to protect the Hollywood child under the age of eighteen in effect encourages the industry to hire young-looking eighteen-year-olds. The unintended result is human casualties like Cummings, who become limbo-ized during the in-between period. "Six months ago, I could not handle it," says Cummings. "It was killing me. I didn't work for almost a year. It would rip my insides out. I would have been less upset if it were personal, but suddenly, I had no control over something that had taken over a great part of my life. There was no one to lash out at, because nobody was directly saying to me, 'You can't have that part.' It was just a basic disinterest of producers and directors to go through the effort of hiring someone under eighteen.

"Then I began to realize I would ride that plateau out. I'd be an 'average person' and turn eighteen, then work again. I'll take a little vacation from acting."

I could almost sense Quinn's pain. She used phrases like 'average person' with forced nonchalance. She is not average, and not even forced retirement should be thought to make her average. She has been a talented actress for years; now she is a talented, unemployable actress. When I interviewed her, she was fourteen and still harbored hopes of "riding out the storm." But for Quinn, the bad weather was just beginning to brew. What would it be like, I had to wonder, if the dark clouds stay overhead until the sunlight of eighteen breaks through?

Says Harrah: "It's going to be a hard, rough, horrible four years."

The fall hits harder the farther the drop. "The greater your degree of celebrity, the greater the pressure and psychological implications of the waning years," says Darryl Hickman.

"It was hard on Darryl," says his brother Dwayne (*The*

Many Loves of Dobie Gillis, 1959–1963), who was unquestionably the less successful *child* actor of the two. "I was dragged into the business because Darryl was in it. I'm glad I worked later, and that the work I did as a child was negligible."

It was not until his early twenties that Dwayne landed the title role in *The Many Loves of Dobie Gillis.* Now a top program executive at CBS, he remains grateful for his early failures, saying, "It's hard to survive as a child celebrity. I was older when it all began to happen. Maybe that's why I'm here [at CBS] now."

For the family breadwinner, the ending can seem especially traumatic. "My teeth fell out and I thought it was all over," author Diana Serra Cary, the silent film child star Baby Peggy told me. "When I was nine and ten, the pressure got very bad because I grew out of any semblance to Baby Peggy. The family moved to a ranch in Wyoming. Then, when I was thirteen, we lost the ranch because of the Depression. I was totally un-equipped to pull us out of the mud, but they couldn't believe I couldn't do it again. So from thirteen to eighteen, I was still trying. I worked at the studios as an extra, or in bit parts. Then when I was around twenty, I broke and ran."

Even without that kind of responsibility, many ex-child stars are equally anxious to revitalize their careers. People like Jay North and Trent Lehman made enough money to remain reasonably comfortable throughout their lifetimes. What is sur-prising is not the avarice, but the burning, almost blind am-bition. "I don't want to live off *The Exorcist* forever," says a determined Linda Blair. "I *will* have a Second Coming."

A few lucky ex-child stars have profited by allowing their im-ages to remain as if frozen in time. Former *Lawrence Welk Show* dancer Bobby Burgess, also a former Mouseketeer, is one of them. "I'm still a kid wearing Mouse ears," he says with pride. *Lawrence Welk* is an adult Mickey Mouse Club." Bobby was a natural dancer. He danced his way over a number of gaps. At five, he found his first dancing partner, a little girl named Judy. The Bobby and Judy team stayed together for three years. Then he performed as a single dancer, until an agent who spotted him on an amateur show asked to represent him as an all-purpose young talent. He was eleven when she managed to book his first toothpaste commercial; it was with Ozzie and Harriet, and after that a lot of other commercials followed. At fourteen, he was cast as a Mouseketeer and began to dance professionally.

After the series folded, Bobby entered college at California State University at Long Beach, but he was not an ambitious student. "I thought I'd be a forest ranger," he recalls, "but you have to have one semester of chemistry. *That was it*, for me." In 1961, he was hired by Lawrence Welk. "I've gone to college part-time for eight years and still haven't finished," he says. "Who would ever have thought the show would last twenty-one years? I love to have security. I love having a series. If the opportunity was there for twenty-one years, why change? I get to do my own choreography, so it's creative. I even get to direct some of my own numbers. When I do my act, I love the reaction of the crowd . . . I do a great lift, spin my partner around and the audience gasps. I keep my body in order, and I stay young." In 1982, however, he had to devise new ways of staying fit; *The Lawrence Welk Show* was canceled. Bobby was crushed. "I wanted to do *The Lawrence Welk Show* until he kicked the bucket. Why not be happy?" Now in his early forties, the former Mouseketeer faces another Gap.

When Jerry Mathers chose to go to high school instead of pursuing acting, he refused to look back, either in anger or in hope. He majored in philosophy at the University of California at Berkeley, and upon graduation found that his biggest philosophical problem was deciding what to do with all his Beaver Cleaver fortune. "I knew I had little business experience," he explains, "and I didn't like the idea of people telling me what to do with my money. So I decided to educate myself. I was a banker for three years. I became an operations officer and a community loan officer." He wanted to invest in property, so he studied and became a real estate agent.

Mathers never expected that, nearly two decades after the

show's end, the American public would become taken with a new wave of Beavermania that has led to national speaking tours, at the rate of roughly $4,000 per booking. Even Mathers' former costar Tony Dow (Beaver's brother Wally on the series) is in demand on the lecture circuit. "Colleges on Saturdays and Sundays were taping *Beaver* and then running the shows," Mathers explains. "Then they'd call us and ask us to appear—without solicitation from us." Mathers and Dow offer a different type of wisdom to America's young scholars than more traditional academic doublebills such as Bob Woodward and John Dean. Instead of behind the scenes at Watergate, they reveal what went on behind the scenes of *Leave It to Beaver*, scraping together whatever anecdotes they are able to remember from twenty years past.

Mathers and Dow, capitalizing on their newfound popularity, placed an ad in *Variety* in the late seventies announcing their availability for a stage play with two male leads. Soon they were booked in a road production of the play *So Long, Stanley*, which ran for one and a half years. "I would get out of the business by choice," says Mathers, "then get back in. If I never worked in the industry again, I'd be a banker or in real estate. But I like acting."

"There's a sense of history now," says casting executive Eve Brandstein (*One Day at a Time, The Facts of Life, Square Pegs*), "because there's been a generation of TV kids who have faded out. When I talk to teenagers today, who recognize the good fortune in their lives, the first thing I hear is that they don't want to be has-beens."

Many of today's child actors are keenly aware that they will soon be over the hill. Some face it courageously. "I don't know if I'll be an actor when I grow up," one ten-year-old boy told a magazine reporter, "because my Mom always tells me there's a time when you just naturally slow down as you get older." By older, he meant thirteen.

"Am I going to college?" one twelve-year-old boy asked this same reporter rhetorically. "My Mom would kill me if I didn't! She always said if acting ever fell short, I should have an occupation to save me. Business administration could always help."

Some children acknowledge the problem begrudgingly. "I'm small for my age," protested eleven-year-old Sydney Penny (NBC-TV's *The Capture of Grizzly Adams*, 1982; ABC-TV's *The Thorn Birds*, 1983), when I pushed her on the point. She is a remarkably gifted and mature dramatic actress. "I want to keep acting. If I do stop working, I'll be busy with school." Clearly, the thought gave her no pleasure. "But I like acting more than school," she confessed.

It is easier, perhaps, not to face it. "They have commercials and movies for all ages," eleven-year-old Jennifer Horton (CBS-TV's *Not in Front of the Children*, 1982) said. She refused to even consider the issue of early retirement. "There's something for everyone," she insisted.

"I wouldn't *think* of stopping in my teens," answered twelve-year-old Shane Butterworth (*Exorcist II: The Heretic*, 1977; *Bad News Bears*, 1979–1980). Could he ever imagine not acting, I asked? He answered with gritty determination, "Not until death do I part."

When I graduated from college with a degree in English, I floated from one odd job to another. Then, tired of the Bay area, I moved back to Los Angeles. Was I seeking a change of scene? Or was I subliminally edging my way back to Hollywood?

I had toyed with the idea of going to graduate school in journalism, but I had toyed with a lot of ideas. Like so many ex-child actors, I was ill-equipped to face a world of harsh economic realities. I had not held a "regular"—i.e., non-acting—job until I was twenty. As if an alien, I roamed around Planet Earth desperate to prove to myself that I had earning power.

Years later, I realized there were deeper psychological and emotional motivations behind the move. I was the not-so-proud possessor of a useless English degree, and I began to feel renewed guilt about leaving the business. Had I thrown away my chances for success?

So many ex-child actors at some point end up probing the soft spots of conviction they once thought so thoroughly firm. When I interviewed Mick Dowd, a former child singer/dancer who had worked at Disney Studios during the fifties and sixties—now an adult actors' agent in his thirties—I was impressed by how precisely he captured the feeling. "Once in a while I'll sing just for fun," he said, "and the comment I always get from friends—which does bring out the guilt—is, 'What a waste! You're so talented!' Then I wonder, 'Is God going to be mad at me because I'm not doing anything with my talent, or does He understand that I wasn't happy?' "

Intellectually, I knew I could never be happy in Hollywood. But I felt I had to wear the hairshirt once more, just to make sure it still hurt. In 1975, at twenty-two years of age, I was accepted as a client by a stage-mother-turned-agent, whose two blonde daughters had been my acting colleagues. "You were a moneymaker," the agent said, "and you just might be again."

Why not give it a try? While waiting for the telephone to ring, I took a job as a hostess at a restaurant nearby Universal Studies. One day, during a hectic lunch hour, I noticed someone who looked familiar waiting for a table.

"Are you Pàm Polifroni, the casting director?" I asked. It was. As a child, I had worked for her numerous times. Now she was the casting director of *The Waltons*.

"I am Andrea Darvi," I told her, thinking she would never recognize me some thirteen years later.

"I feel so old!" she cried. "You were just a wee little thing last time I saw you!"

I told her I was now twenty-two, and she seemed to believe me. At least she did not ask to examine my driver's license. Two weeks later, my agent called to tell me that Polifroni had requested that I audition for a part on *The Waltons*. I was flattered, although I knew I had no more chance of playing a midwestern farm girl than an Austrian Von Trapp family singer. I was twelve years older and had not gotten any less Mediterranean.

I went to the interview. I had been taught since childhood never to turn down a chance to be seen. Even if you knew you would not get the part, simply showing up might lead to something else. Someone could be casting *The Waltons* one day, and *Hawaii Five-O* the next.

The Waltons interview seemed grotesque. I had forgotten what these calls were like, and the great labors people took to look and dress the part. There were girls wearing long prairie-style skirts and old-fashioned blouses. Obviously, they were casting both a mother and a daughter. There were older, grandmotherly types wearing their hair in buns on the backs of their heads. I almost always played orphans, so I could not imagine where I fit in. But like everyone else in the room, I studied the coveted two-page scene for which at least forty people were crammed into the casting office.

I was finally called into the audition room. Polifroni introduced me to the group of men seated next to her, "This girl was the best child actress—I mean, the best!"

I did not get the *Waltons* part, of course. But I got the epitaph I had always wanted, even if it may have been better than I actually deserved.

Seven years later, one day in 1982, I drove to Burbank Studios to interview Earl Hamner, creator and narrator of *The Waltons*. I figured he would know a lot about working with kids. Sitting in a French restaurant near the studio, Hamner asked me if I was still acting. I was stunned by the question, though I assured him that I was not. How did he know I had been a child actress? I had presented myself to him as a working journalist.

Over lunch, we talked about "series kids." He liked to sit in at *Waltons* interviews, he told me, since the series' subject matter was based on his own life, and therefore close to his emotions. Then it dawned on me! Earl Hamner thought of me as an actress because he had been one of those men sitting in on that *Waltons* call I attended at the age of twenty-two.

I generally have a terrific memory. Why had I forgotten about auditioning for Hamner? Had I suppressed the memory of that scene at Burbank Studios? Then I speculated on another reason for my temporary amnesia. Like most ex-child actors, I had underestimated what I had accomplished. Since the teen years, I had come to view myself as little more than a fallen actress, deprecating all that preceded that fall. While a self-destructive posture, it was also a self-protective one. It is understandably difficult to conceive how an industry could so abruptly reject you if your contribution to it had once been so important. In order to break all ties with the past, I had to make failures out of my successes. To be free, I had to view acting as something ultimately trivial, virtually nonexistent; something never gained, rather than something gained only to be lost. On February 30, 1967, I had written in my diary, "It all boils down to this: I'm an actress, not a nobody. I love it so much. It's my only sense of belonging. All I want, all I need now is a job. I think I was destined for show business."

And I was so sure of myself then.

Fifteen years later, I was behaving as if child actress Andrea Darvi had never existed. Both attitudes were extremes; both were wrong. But both were understandable. At least, I have finally come to understand them now, nearly two decades after my final Hollywood bow.

Children will always play a leading role in the entertainment world. The Hollywood dream machine is not about to stop churning out the kinds of characters that for decades have helped boost the Nielsens and box office sales. For their part, parents and children will inevitably be lured by the incomparable glamour and excitement of Hollywood. It would be foolish to expect the nature of the entertainment industry, or of human beings, to change. But perhaps the time will come when many more parents will be far more cautious, and ultimately unwilling, before subjecting their children to this madness.

I suppose I came out of that mad drama stronger and smarter

for the experience. As a close friend once put it, I have had the enormous bonus of living two lives, rather than one. But that first life was so special, and awful, that it continues to dominate the second. Two lives are not necessarily twice the best. One—either one—would have been more than enough.

There was one thing fundamentally wrong with the first life; it ended. That is when my anguish began. My specialness faded as quickly and inexplicably as it had arrived. I was nothing more I had been led to believe than the sum total of my roles, and as they became fragments of an ever-distant past, my present became ever more inconsequential. My life seemed as empty and meaningless as a blank television screen after the last credit has rolled by.

Having once been a child actress, I feel that society did me a grave injustice by forcing me to become a full-fledged adult.

Index